THE WAY OF THE WORD

What the Bible says

How it applies to you

How you can obey

BRYAN SMITH

BIBLE
MODULAR
SERIES

BJU PRESS

Greenville, South Carolina

T his textbook was written by members of the faculty and staff of Bob Jones University. Standing for the "old-time religion" and the absolute authority of the Bible since 1927, Bob Jones University is the world's leading fundamental Christian university. The staff of the University is devoted to educating Christian men and women to be servants of Jesus Christ in all walks of life.

Providing unparalleled academic excellence, Bob Jones University prepares its students through its offering of over 120 majors, while its fervent spiritual emphasis prepares their minds and hearts for service and devotion to the Lord Jesus Christ.

▶ If you would like more information about the spiritual and academic opportunities available at Bob Jones University, please call **1-800-BJ-AND-ME (1-800-252-6363)**. **www.bju.edu**

NOTE:
The fact that materials produced by other publishers may be referred to in this volume does not constitute an endorsement of the content or theological position of materials produced by such publishers. Any references and ancillary materials are listed as an aid to the student or the teacher and in an attempt to maintain the accepted academic standards of the publishing industry.

The Way of the Word

Bryan Smith, M.A.

© 2000 BJU Press
Greenville, South Carolina 29614

Printed in the United States of America

ISBN 978-1-57924-323-4

15 14 13 12 11 10 9 8 7 6 5 4

CONTENTS

First Steps

1

Psalm 119:1-8

Growing or Backsliding

I had no reason to think anything was wrong. The phone often rang around suppertime. My brother picked up the receiver with an ordinary "Hello," and we soon figured out that it was one of our good friends from out of town. But after the expected greetings, my brother became disturbingly quiet. When he hung up the phone, he looked sobered and a little angry. "That was Cindy—Tony's in trouble," he started. We all instinctively braced ourselves for whatever was coming next. "Tony confessed that he is living a lie and that for the last month he's been having an affair with someone in his church." *How could he do that?* I thought. *Wasn't Tony happily married and faithfully serving the Lord? He taught in his Christian school and regularly preached in chapel.*

During the ensuing weeks, Tony shared with his family what had been going on in his soul. Then this puzzling tragedy began to make sense. One confession he made stood out far above the rest, expressing the root of his failure: "I haven't read my Bible for *two years.*" Though he was busy for the Lord, his spirit had become comatose, lulled to sleep by a dangerous neglect of God's Word. "At first," he explained, "it was hard to preach in chapel, knowing I hadn't even had my devotions. But after a while it got easier." During those years of uninterrupted backsliding, many things got easier: a wandering eye, inviting smiles, the purposeful touch, and shameless words. Having ignored God for so long, Tony was easily trapped in a web of adultery.

We've often heard that succinct proverb, penned in countless Bible flyleaves, "Either this book will keep you from sin, or sin will keep you from this book." Perhaps the saying is so often repeated because it is so often proved true. If you do not regularly meet with God, you will in time become insensitive to His holy presence. Once you no longer sense His purifying gaze, you will stop fearing sin. Then life can quickly erode into a slippery slide toward ruin. Because of this danger, the apostle Peter warned his readers, "Pass the time of your sojourning here in fear" (I Pet. 1:17). Fear alone, however, is not enough. Therefore, Peter gave an additional command, "Desire the sincere milk of the word that ye may grow thereby" (I Pet. 2:2). Rather than *sliding* into Satan's traps, we are to *grow* in God's way by daily feeding on His Word. There is no surer way to keep from being devoured by the Adversary.

Just What We Need?

Despite the obvious dangers, many of us still neglect our Bibles. We often complain that the Bible isn't exciting and that it doesn't seem relevant to our needs. After all, the Bible was written a long time ago by people we don't even know. Furthermore, it isn't exactly easy to understand. But what a thrill it would be if God would speak to us through spectacular visions! We would be able to interact with Him about His will, understanding more of His message. Such interaction would also be fresh, exciting, and personal. If God communicated in this way, every Christian would have just what he needed—and wanted—to grow spiritually, right?

Certainty for the Soul

The apostle Peter, who received such revelations, disagreed with this thinking. He had actually seen Christ's glory on the mount of transfiguration (II Pet. 1:16-19), yet he confidently affirmed that all Christians possess "a more sure word of prophecy" than his mountaintop experience. Then he explains, "For the prophecy came not in old time by the will of man: but holy men of God spake as they were moved by the Holy Ghost" (v. 21). As God's inspired, preserved Word, the Bible is more reliable than dreams or visions. Why? The Word is not dependent on human frailties such as the powers of eyesight, hearing, or memory. If God revealed Himself only in those ways, we would constantly wonder whether we really heard Him right or got all the information just as He gave it. But the Word is flawless and preserved. Anytime we think we have forgotten or misunderstood His communication, we are free to go back and check that inerrant, unchanging message. Though a vision may be more spectacular, the written Word of God is far better for meeting our needs.

Power to Change

Those who think the Bible is boring compared to stunning revelations fail to realize the power of this book. God's Word, not visions and miracles, has changed the world. Though miraculous signs confirmed the apostles' teaching, the work that changed the world was simply the proclamation of the written Word. When the apostolic age closed, the signs and wonders came to an end, but God's Word continued to be preached and read—and continued to change lives. The fiercest Roman persecutions took place in the two centuries after the apostles, yet during that time the church experienced its most startling growth. Some have estimated that by the early fourth century Christians in the Roman Empire numbered ten million—roughly ten percent of the Empire. What were these millions of conversions like? Take the following paragraph as an example.

The year A.D. 386 found Augustine a broken man, living in Milan. He had squandered his days in immorality, but the prayers of his mother followed him, as did the Holy Spirit's conviction. Previously, while living in Northern Africa, he had sought relief from a number of sources. One that had occupied many of his efforts was the false religion of Manichaeism. In time, however, this lie had lost its grip on him because it failed to answer adequately his perceptive questions. At last he moved to Milan,

Think About It!

The spread of Christianity stands in stark contrast to the spread of Islam. The history of the church from Pentecost to the rise of Emperor Constantine records a series of fierce persecutions. The opposition came as no surprise to believers, for their Lord had warned them of the world's hatred. But rather than empowering the saints with weapons for war to help them in this wicked world, Christ gave them His Spirit and His words (Matt. 10:19; Acts 1:8). Despite daunting opposition, Christianity multiplied until it saturated the empire and persuaded the emperor himself to be converted. Indeed, "the blood of the Christians is the seed of the church."

The nature of Islam's spread was entirely different. This religion had its birth in A.D. 610 when Muhammad began experiencing visions of Allah. In just a little more than a century, by 732, Islam had spread over Persia, Iraq, Palestine, Northern Africa, and Spain. What was its secret? *Jihad*—holy war. The sword secured every new victory. Indeed, the blood of Muhammed's enemies is the seed of Islam.

---

where he taught logic. There he became intrigued by the gospel preaching of a minister named Ambrose. Augustine longed to believe that gospel, but he could not give his whole heart to it be-

Augustine

cause he was enslaved to his sin. One night, tormented by his seemingly helpless state, he wept alone in a garden. Suddenly, his sobs were interrupted by two commands pressing his soul: "Tolle, lege" (Take up, read). He grabbed a copy of the Scripture and providentially opened to Romans 13:13-14: "not in chambering and wantonness, not in strife and envying. But put ye on the Lord Jesus Christ, and make not provision for the flesh." He saw no vision; he simply wept and read God's Word. But the Lord was clearly at work, for there in the garden, Augustine submitted to the gospel. He left his life of sin and eventually became one of the most influential Christian leaders and theologians in history.

Where's the Power? Where's the *Faith?*

America is certainly no stranger to the Word of God. Never before have the Scriptures and books about the Bible been as prevalent as they are today in this country. Surprisingly, however, it seems that the more religious books and Bibles are published, the more our culture repudiates biblical teaching. Why isn't the Bible changing our world as we know it can? Has God failed us? Certainly not. The reason most people have never been changed by the Bible is that they do not really believe the Bible. Test your own faith in the Scripture by seriously considering the following questions.

1. **Do you study your Bible regularly?**

2. **Have you read your Bible today?**

3. **If you did, how long did you spend in God's Word?**

4. **How has your life changed in the last week because of something you've discovered in your personal Bible study?**

If you didn't fare very well on these four questions, you may be protesting, "I may not read the Bible much, but that doesn't mean I don't believe it." While that may seem like a legitimate statement, it is in fact quite contradictory. If we are convinced that meditating day and night in God's law will make us prosper in His chosen way (Ps. 1), we will prioritize our lives to ensure effective Bible study every day. "But I just don't have the time to read my Bible every day." Strange. We don't say that we're too busy to eat. No matter how tight our schedules get, we never go a day without food. Why? Eating is important to us—you get the point? *People who do not regularly study their Bibles fail to do so because of a lack of interest that is due to a lack of faith.*

Take the Challenge

Do you believe that the Bible is God's Word for *you?* Then treat it as such by giving your life to understanding and living its teachings. Don't fancy that a lesser commitment will do. The fact is that, though Bible-study-made-easy books abound, the Bible is not easy to read or study. By God's design it abounds with challenges for the reader. Through those challenges the Lord is testing us to see if we will forsake our selfishness and our unbelief. *Tolle, lege*—you'll be glad you did.

Three Daily Tasks

If you take the challenge of living in submission to God's Word, there are three specific tasks you will face daily. Your first responsibility is to comprehend *what the Bible meant* to its original audience. Here, you are trying to understand the text as well as the author did, or as well as the author intended his readers to understand it. The technical name for this task is *exegesis*, but we will also use the term **exploration** to describe this phase of interpreting the Bible. Since the Bible is also God's Word for people today, there is a second very important step in biblical interpretation, **application.** This involves discerning *what the significance is* of the ancient meaning. Carefully note the difference between exploration and application. A person states the result of *exploration* when he says, "Romans 1:16 states that Paul was not ashamed of the gospel." But he expresses an *application* when he says, "Romans 1:16 teaches me that I should not be ashamed of the gospel." Once you have explored and applied the text, interpretation is done, but interacting with God has just begun. You are not walking in God's way until you are living in **obedience**—doing the application that you have discovered. Our discussion of obedience at the end of this book will focus on the key question, *How can we submit to scriptural applications?*

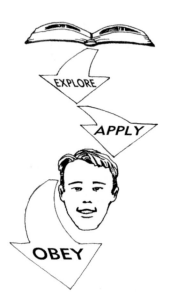

More Than Reading, More Than Believing

I personally can attest to the changing power of God's Word. I was thirteen when I began reading the Bible regularly, and I was amazed at the change that took place by simply "taking up and reading." In time, however, I became frustrated. With all my heart I believed what I was reading, but I sensed I was missing far more than I understood. The Bible seemed more like a puzzling maze than a road to God. Though I had read certain parts numerous times, I never seemed to understand them any better because I lacked a solid foundation in biblical interpretation. In time and with struggle, that foundation was laid, and through that experience I discovered that grasping the Bible's teachings requires more than faith and casual reading. The full blessings of the Scripture are for those who take the time to understand the way of the Word. Learning how the Bible communicates its truths is at times mentally demanding, but it offers a rich relationship with God as its reward.

Getting Started

When you are getting started in Bible study, the most important thing to know is not the "ins and outs" of biblical interpretation. You must first settle more basic questions: *What do you want to accomplish?* and *How will you go about doing it?* Do not underestimate the importance of planning your Bible study and prayer. Worship in the Bible is an orderly, well-structured experience. The apostle Paul commanded the Corinthian Christians to conduct their public worship "decently and in order" (I Cor. 14:40). Paul's prayers and the many prayers in the Psalms likewise show careful organization. If we follow the example of

GET THE BIG PICTURE

George Müller

In his autobiography George Müller (1805-1898) states some lessons he learned about communing with God through Bible reading and prayer.

> I saw more clearly than ever, that the first great and primary business to which I ought to attend every day was, to have my soul happy in the Lord. . . . I saw that the most important thing I had to do was to give myself to the reading of the word of God, and to meditation on it. . . . After a very few minutes my soul has been led to confession, or to thanksgiving, or to intercession, or to supplication; so that, though I did not, as it were, give myself to *prayer* but to *meditation*, yet it turned almost immediately more or less into prayer.

believers who effectively communed with God, we will pursue God according to a plan.

Not all of the following guidelines are biblical mandates. Some are simply methods that have worked well for others. But before you dismiss any of them, consider that many people have successfully grown in the Lord while following a plan such as this one.

The Goal and Non-Goals

Pursue God

The Bible is God's revelation by which the Lord shows how He is reversing the curse that fell on all mankind. Therefore, the goal of studying this book must be to experience the reversal of that curse. Since that reversal is essentially a restored relationship with God, your goal in studying the Word of God must be *a vital communion with God that produces a changed life.* We read the Bible not to know more *about* God but to *know God* and to become more like Him. Whatever additional goals you may have must contribute to this fellowship. You also must consistently guard against illegitimate goals invading your Bible study.

Avoid Conscience Salving

Do not fall into the trap of using the Bible to salve your conscience. We all realize the importance of reading the Bible every day. But if we are not careful, we can make our time with God a superficial ritual for experiencing a release from guilt. The danger here is twofold. First, we may stop growing spiritually because we think all that God wants from us is a few minutes looking at words on a page. Second, we may stop reading His Word altogether because we end up viewing that time as a cold "sacrament" that will not meet our spiritual needs. The question that really matters is not "Have I read my Bible today?" but rather "Have I met with God today?"

Avoid Knowledge for Knowledge's Sake

Do not study the Bible just to be a scholar. Certainly, there is nothing wrong with being a scholar. The amazing prevalence of God's Word in our own language testifies to the blessings of scholarship. Nevertheless, longing to achieve biblical expertise simply for the sake of having that expertise is a most dangerous kind of pride. God has given us His Word so that we might know Him—not so that we might be smart. Usually, such an academic interest results from studying the Word without submitting to the Word. If we accurately perceive God's message but do not obey it, either we will stop reading our Bibles or our goal will become gaining knowledge for knowledge's sake. Study the Word of God, but don't stop there. Obey the commands that you discover in your study.

Closely related to this attitude of academic detachment is the dangerous tendency to be critical of the text. At times you will need to investigate what seems to be a contradiction in the Bible. However, you must remember that every word has been "given by inspiration of God" (II Tim. 3:16). Consequently, a confident submission to the Bible's accuracy must rule your spirit. You cannot stand in judgment over the text and hear God's voice; rather, you must let the text stand in judgment of you. By the way, if you approach these apparent contradictions with this attitude, you will find that the Bible vindicates itself every time.

Avoid Looking-for-a-Verse

Finally, beware of reading your Bible simply to find "a verse for the day." Though God often reveals important truths to people in just one sentence, regularly searching for only a verse will prove misleading. God did not write the Bible as an anthology of verses meant to be individual "blessers." He wrote a library of sixty-six books, each having its own theme. To read the Bible the way it is meant to be read, you must look for the message of each book. Therefore, this course discusses only one method of Bible study—book studies. Though there are certainly other legitimate methods, the book study should be the believer's primary method.

Tools

The number of tools designed to help people in their Bible study and prayer could be described as *legion*. This section is not intended to be an exhaustive list of these kinds of tools—such a goal would be impractical, not to mention unattainable. For our purposes in this course, the following aids stand out as especially helpful and are therefore worthy of our consideration.

Wide-Margin Bible

Of course, the most important tool for communing with God is a good copy of the Scriptures. Your best investment will probably not be a study Bible filled with footnotes explaining the text. Though this may seem like a good investment, it will most likely hinder your Bible study progress if you use it as your primary Bible. Such a Bible floods you with information before you are ready to assimilate it. Consequently study Bibles tend to distract readers, not guide them. You should

Martin Luther

Martin Luther (1483-1546) was so mightily used by God during the Reformation that he could be described as the "Man of the Millennium." Though known for his bold opposition to error, Luther was also a man who through quiet meditation knew God—as the following advice he once gave indicates.

> When your heart has been warmed by such recitation to yourself (of the Ten Commandments, the words of Christ, etc.) and is intent upon the matter, kneel or stand . . . and speak . . . "Our Father who art, etc.," through the whole prayer, word for word. . . . To this day I suckle at the Lord's Prayer like a child, and as an old man eat and drink from it and never get my fill. It is the very best prayer. . . . It is surely evident that a real Master composed and taught it.

investigate the text itself first; then, once you have clearly formed your own questions regarding the passage, you should look in a study Bible or commentary for answers to specific questions.

Ideally, your primary Bible should be a "warehouse" to store the observations and conclusions of your study. Therefore your best investment will probably be a wide-margin Bible. Such a Bible will give you plenty of room to underline key words and place brief explanations in the margin. Thus your conclusions from daily study will always be readily available.

Prayer Notebook

A prayer notebook can be a great help in developing an effective prayer life. Not only does such a book provide a place to list prayer requests, but it can also remind us to pray well. When the disciples said, "Lord, teach us to pray," Christ responded by giving them what is now called the Lord's Prayer (Matt. 6:9-13). This model prayer should guide every believer each day as he endeavors to pray. Consider writing out the Lord's Prayer in your notebook, praying through it daily. Of course, you do not need to pray it word-for-word, but you should use it as a guide to direct your requests toward *God's* desires. You may also include a schedule for praying through certain psalms regularly. Many psalms are model prayers that God has given us to follow. If you have a schedule, you can pray through these several times in a year.

Your prayer list should include long-standing requests (salvation of certain people, spiritual growth for yourself and others, needs of missionaries, and so forth). Your prayer list needs to include more immediate concerns as well. Therefore, use a notebook small enough (preferably small enough to fit in your pocket) to carry with you. If you do this, you will be able to jot down at a moment's notice requests that people ask you to remember throughout the day. Be sure to keep track of when you began praying for a particular need. Then record when God answers that prayer. Your faith will grow as you notice how many prayers the Lord answers weekly.

Journals

In addition to these tools, you may want to use two journals. The first may function as a study journal, in which you jot down your thoughts and conclusions as you study. In places this book will be quite messy because it will record your first attempts at reasoning through passages of Scripture. Though the journal may not look pretty, you should keep it—even when you can no longer use it—because it will record your Bible study conclusions as well as the reasoning that led to those conclusions.

The second journal can be used for personal notations. Here you can record your summaries of the text as you read. As you discover God's Word and record the meaning, you should also be careful to jot down applications of that meaning to your own life. Primarily, this journal is a tool for solidifying what the Lord is teaching you personally from the Scripture. You will remember lessons you have written down much better than lessons you note only mentally.

C. H. Spurgeon

Charles Haddon Spurgeon (1834-1892) was probably the most famous English preacher in the second half of the nineteenth century. To this day his insightful, eloquent sermons minister rich blessing to God's people. Through his extensive work with the Bible, he learned the value of commentaries.

> In order to be able to expound the Scriptures . . . you will need to be familiar with the commentators. . . . If you are of that opinion [that commentaries are not helpful], pray remain so, for you are not worth the trouble of conversion. . . . It seems odd, that certain men who talk so much of what the Holy Spirit reveals to themselves, should think so little of what he has revealed to others.

Bible Encyclopedias and Commentaries

Bible encyclopedias and commentaries are indeed helpful, but they must be used properly. You should go to these tools only after you have investigated the text yourself and have well-formed questions in your mind. Far too often students of Scripture go to commentaries simply because using them seems like "the thing to do." Consequently they wander aimlessly through pages of informative—but not helpful—material. You should use these tools only to help answer questions that you have discovered you cannot answer for yourself.

Bible encyclopedias offer good information concerning books of the Bible generally. They also deal with a host of important Bible-related topics. Each topic or Bible book will be discussed in alphabetical order so that the information is easy to find. Most articles are only a few pages in length.

Individual commentaries give the reader more particular, verse-by-verse information on books of the Bible. If your question regards the interpretation of a particular word, phrase, verse, or even paragraph, the commentary is the tool you need. The introductory section to most commentaries offers helpful information about the historical background, overall message, and special interpretive problems of the book.

A word of caution is in order. By no means are all commentaries and Bible encyclopedias of equal value. Some do not focus on the issues that are truly helpful. Therefore, you should avoid those books. Others may deal with such issues, but, because the books' authors do not believe that the Bible is the Word of God, you should also stay away from these reference tools. Your teacher will have a list to help you find valuable commentaries and encyclopedias.

A Good Plan

Preparation

 When you first sit down with your Bible, you will need to prepare your mind and heart. The best way to begin this preparation is by praying for the Holy Spirit's guidance. Ask Him to reveal His message to you and show you what you need to change. Usually after this brief prayer, a further step of preparation is helpful. Try singing—ever so quietly if necessary—a hymn or two from a hymnal to focus your soul on things above.

Reading the Scripture

 Many people learn little while they read the Scripture because they read without purpose. An important way to guide your investigation is to jot down thoughts in your personal journal while you read. Never leave a passage of Scripture without attempting to summarize the content. This will stimulate your mind to think through God's message and guide you to applications. Often you will find that after reading a portion you can think of no application for your life. However, if you will summarize the content in such cases, application ideas will usually start flowing. After the summary statements, record applications of how you should act, think, or pray because of something in the passages you have read.

As you have time, you should use the study journal to record your more technical and thorough investigations. At this point, nothing more needs to be said about using this journal. The majority of our study after this chapter will deal with detailed analysis involving the study journal.

Praying

Now you are ready to spend some time in concentrated prayer. Begin by asking the Lord to give you the grace to obey the applications that He has shown you. Remember to spend some time praying through biblical prayers. These prayers will direct your heart toward praising God and making requests in a biblical manner.

As you work through your prayer list, be sure to pray for your family, your church and its leadership, missionaries, and unsaved people you know. However, you must be careful not to overload this prayer time. As you begin, you will tend to make huge prayer lists. But if you do not divide your requests over several days or somehow keep each day's list to a reasonable limit, you will eventually frustrate yourself and may even quit meeting with God altogether. Starting out, it is far better to pray a little, but consistently, than to pray much for only a few days. In time your ability to pray for longer periods will increase.

Accountability

If you spend time in the Word at the beginning of the day, then in the evening you can come back to your "quiet place" and make yourself accountable by reflecting on the day. In the quietness of your room or study, pull out your personal journal and review that morning's summaries and application notes. Then summarize the activities of the day, relating how you implemented the applications God gave you that morning. Record opportunities to witness, moments of victory over sin, or success in challenging others to be godly. Be sure, however, to record your failures as well.

This practice will give you a much better idea of where you stand spiritually. It will also encourage you as you see yourself grow in the Lord. Just as keeping a prayer list that records God's many answers will strengthen your faith in prayer, so keeping track of what you do with God's communication from day to day will encourage you to continue growing in His grace. Sometimes Christians stop growing because they misunderstand the nature of growth. God grows Christlike character slowly over a long period of time. The soul that makes no attempt to mark that growth will most likely fail to perceive God's gracious working. Practicing this kind of accountability will also guard your soul against apathy. The subtle sin of backsliding is much easier to notice if you keep track of your spiritual progress. The unconcerned Christian will think that such a task is a wearisome burden, but the committed believer will view the exercise as indispensable.

What's Ahead?

In the next four chapters we will discuss exploring different parts of Scripture. The key skill that we are attempting to develop is simply a thoughtful reading of the text, which has as its goal a solid understanding of the biblical author's intended meaning. This task is simple, but not easy. The process that we are going to describe need not be the plan you follow every time you meet with the Lord. However, thoughtful reading skills are developed through rigorous study. Therefore the more you take time to study the Scriptures, the more profitable your daily Bible reading will become.

Review Questions

Write *T* in the blank if the statement accurately reflects the content of this chapter and *F* if it does not.

_____1. Though certain passages are difficult, the bulk of Scripture is easy to read and interpret.

_____2. The goal of Bible study is to learn more about God.

_____3. A study Bible can be helpful, but if a person uses it as his primary Bible, it will most likely hinder his progress in Bible study.

Choose the answer that best represents the content of this chapter.

_____4. The Bible (not dreams or visions) is just what we need to grow spiritually because

    A. the Bible requires a level of faith and devotion that dreams and visions do not.

    B. the Bible preserves God's message in an unchangeable form and evidences an incredible power to change lives.

    C. dreams and visions come from Satan.

    D. the Bible is inspired.

_____5. Martin Luther found that __ helped him greatly in learning how to pray.

    A. the Lord's Prayer (Matt. 6:9-13)

    B. Christ's High-Priestly prayer (John 17)

    C. Paul's prayer in Ephesians 3:14-21

    D. David's prayer of contrition (Ps. 51)

_____6. Carefully planning your Bible study and prayer time

    A. directly contradicts the examples of worship in the Bible.

    B. will inevitably lead to formalism and deadness in your devotions.

    C. is the main reason people get discouraged while trying to establish devotions as a daily habit.

    D. is an important part of meeting with God and must not be underestimated.

Short Answer

7. According to this chapter, what is God's ordained means for escaping Satan's traps?

8. Why is the Bible not changing our world today?

9. What are the three actions each person must engage in if he wants to grow through God's Word?

10. What is the goal of Bible study?

11. Why are believers who do not regularly read their Bibles especially susceptible to failure in times of temptation?

12. Contrast the triumph of Christianity in the Roman world with the triumph of Islam in the Middle East and Africa. What does that contrast imply about the Bible?

13. How would you respond to a person who says that he does not need to read the Bible because God speaks directly to him while he prays?

14. Summarize what is involved in "getting started" in Bible study.

Project

Follow the suggestions outlined in "Getting Started" for seven days as you read the Bible and meet with God.

*E*xplore!—Charting the Way of the Word

2

Proverbs 2:1-5

*D*id God Say *That?*

Though Melissa was a devoted Christian, she was struggling with a number of difficult problems. When I met her, she had just come through a long period of family crises, and though the Lord had delivered her, she still had to deal with quite a bit of emotional baggage. One of her most discouraging struggles was loneliness—she was middle-aged and single. More than lonely, though, she was confused.

"When I was going through all that trouble with my family," she shared at one point, "the Lord gave me a verse that said I would get married. I'm confident that He promised to give me a husband. But He hasn't done it." I was more than a little stunned by this revelation, but I quickly collected my thoughts because I wanted to know what verse in the Bible could be so explicit. "In Isaiah 43:4," she continued, "God told me, 'I have loved thee: therefore will I give men for thee.'" Then that stunned feeling returned, but for a different reason.

Did God "give" Melissa that verse? Any honest student of Isaiah would have to say *No.* Why? The text has never meant what she was claiming, and the text cannot mean what it has never meant. Isaiah 43 records God's encouragement for the nation of Judah. There He draws a parallel between His miraculous deliverance of His people during the Exodus and His future restoration of this wayward, afflicted nation. Though they would undergo the

21

Lord's fierce wrath, He would be merciful. Just as God had slaughtered the Egyptians to deliver His people in the Exodus, so He promises in Isaiah 43:4 that He will "give" (as in *sacrifice*) many other "men" in order to restore His people. There are no wedding bells in this verse—the men in this passage are going to die. To find in this text a reference to future marriage possibilities is a dangerous twisting of the author's intent. If this kind of interpretation were legitimate, anyone could make any Bible passage mean anything.

But why did this verse "leap off the page" to Melissa (and out of its historical and written context)? She wanted it to. Probably the day she read that passage, she was feeling especially lonely. When she picked up her Bible, she was hoping God would communicate with her about that loneliness. Then she saw the word that encapsulated what she was thinking about—*men*. Voilà! A promise from the Lord.

Not everyone would agree with my assessment of Melissa's problem. Some may insist that since she was sincere, her "looking for a verse" was completely harmless. Such a defense, however, is simply untenable—harm was done. Nevertheless, many believers are slow to condemn such Bible study because it seems that God has often used this method to direct His children. However, the fact that the Lord does stoop to communicate through such means is a testimony to His grace, not to the validity of the method. God honors faith. When people come to the Word believing it is God's revelation and that it will meet their needs, His heart is moved to help them. But the Lord will not always so stoop. He cannot. Such a method of Bible study takes the form of Scripture as its authority but ends up making the interpreter the authority. In other words, this approach to the Bible teaches that whatever the reader wants the text to mean it means.

So what was Melissa's mistake? *Her fundamental error was skipping exegesis.* She believed that the Bible was God's Word for her personally, but she was in too much of a hurry to take the time to ask, "What did this mean to the original audience?" or "How did the author understand these words?" Though it takes time and effort, interpretation must begin with exploring the author's intended meaning. If we do not begin there, we will never know whether what we have discovered in the Scripture has come from God or from our imagination.

What's Exegesis All About?

You Can Do This "Exploring"

Interpretation, exegesis—the words themselves sound intimidating. Perhaps they make you think of old men in small, dark cells chasing prepositions around the room. Or maybe exegesis reminds you of linguistic quarrels: "I know the English says *yes,* but the Greek says *no!*" The point is that most of us find biblical exegesis intimidating because we think interpretation requires highly specialized skills. But Moses Stuart, an insightful scholar from the nineteenth century, came to a very different conclusion: "All men are, and ever have been, in reality, good and true interpreters of each other's language." That's right; you are a fine interpreter. You've been honing your skills ever since you were born. Let me prove this to you by asking you a few questions about the book you are presently reading, or perhaps I should say *interpreting.*

1. Who wrote this book?

2. Where did this book come from (who published it)?

3. What is this book about? (Try to state it in one sentence.)

4. Why do you think this book was written?

5. How does the author develop his theme (what is the structure of this book)?

Moses Stuart

Some have called Moses Stuart (1780-1852) "the Father of Biblical Learning in America." After pastoring for four years in Connecticut, he became the professor of sacred literature at Andover Theological Seminary, Andover, Massachusetts. During his four decades at Andover, he published almost forty books and brochures and taught 1,500 ministers and seventy professors or college presidents. One of those ministers was America's first foreign missionary, Adoniram Judson—who was converted while taking classes at Andover.

Stuart, however, was more than a gifted teacher and writer. He was a man who knew and loved the Lord Jesus Christ. At his funeral, the following expression of devotion was attributed to him: "I ask for no other privilege on earth, but to make known the efficacy of [Christ's] death; and none in heaven, but to be associated with those who ascribe salvation to his blood. Amen."

Knowing Your Circle

If you think that the questions on the previous page are too easy, think again. These are the kinds of questions that Bible interpreters ask every time they come to a text, difficult or easy. Then why devote an entire book to Bible study? If it's really that easy, a person should just read the Bible, and the meaning will be obvious, right? Wrong.

Interpreting correctly is as easy as breathing—*provided the interpreter is operating within his own circle of knowledge.* As soon as a person gets outside that circle, his ability to investigate effectively begins to fall apart. Moses Stuart himself, only a few sentences after calling all men good interpreters, admitted that people cannot understand a text beyond their circle of knowledge. You probably did a fine job on the previous five questions, but consider this paragraph.

> Peter answered the Lord's question confidently, "Thou art the Christ, the Son of the living God." Note carefully that Peter's syntactical structure is very emphatic. He uses

both the emphatic personal pronoun *(su)* along with the present indicative linking verb *(ei)*. Note also how emphatic the predicate is: every element is articular, no part is anartharous. Though our Lord's response may seem to validate certain pontifical claims, the grammar of His reply clearly indicates otherwise: Christ employs here a future perfect periphrastic, viewing the future event as already completed.

Well, how did you do on this one? Probably not quite as well as you did with the first pages of this book. By now you probably know the reason too. The paragraph above is outside your circle of knowledge. To understand it, you have to know some rather technical grammatical terms as well as possess a working knowledge of Koine Greek. If, however, your circle of knowledge included this information, you could understand these words just as well as the person who wrote them.

Now consider God's Word. The fact is that many passages of Scripture have elements that are beyond most people's circle of knowledge. So to do a good job of interpreting the Bible, you must learn how to broaden that circle, and that is what the study of exegesis is all about—teaching you how to broaden your circle of knowledge so that you can interpret a given text of Scripture.

Stretching Your Circle

Basically, stretching your circle of knowledge comes down to one skill—asking the right questions of the text. This is how you understand any piece of communication. When your teacher says, "I am now going to tell you what will be on the upcoming test," your mind immediately prepares itself for the rest of the review by asking, "What will be on the test?" As the teacher keeps speaking, your mind continually asks that question until it is satisfied. When, however, we approach a text outside our circle of knowledge, we usually get frustrated and forget how to interpret.

For example, in the earlier incomprehensible paragraph, you probably got so confused after a few sentences that your mind stopped asking the right questions, which you naturally and constantly are asking as you read this book. The moment you stop asking the right questions is the moment good interpretation stops.

So what are these questions? They are easy to remember; five of them start with *w* and one starts with *h*: *where, when, who, what, why,* and *how.* The first four questions concern matters of observation: facts about the historical context *(where, when, who)* and facts about the written context *(what).* The last two questions are more interpretive because they take place on a higher level: *why* the author is saying what he is saying and *how* he has structured his facts and arguments to say it.

Genre and Exploring

Before we actually get into the specifics of biblical exploration, we need to consider another complicating factor—genre. *Genre* is a French word that simply means "kind." In English we use it to refer to "kinds of literature." Poetry, sermon, and narrative are all genres because they are types of literature. The genre that a book is written in profoundly affects how we are going to ask our questions. For example, note how the same words communicate different ideas in the following two examples. The first is a narrative; the second is a poem.

> Jonathan gleefully entered the room, glad to share the happy news with his mother. "Guess what, Mom." Kindly, yet with sufficient severity, she reminded him, "*Shut the door.* I know you have something exciting to tell me, but no news is so wonderful that it excuses bad manners." Thus corrected, he closed the door.

> Black as night blows evil's curse,
> With vicious zeal it chilled mankind.
> "Who dare doubt or make demand?"
> So hearts grow cold and darken worse.

Arise bright Son and bleach offense.
The Blackness send to own his lair;
Our house be light, and dark no more.
Then *shut the door;* our hearts enclose.

Though the italicized words are the same, they ultimately refer to very different actions. Why? The genres are different. When we read simple prose, we expect straightforward, plain communication. But when reading poetry, we expect many figures of speech, producing rich imagery.

Get Ready!

In the next three chapters, we will discuss the three major genres found in the Bible. In each chapter we will note how the conventions of a given genre affect the way the author communicates his ideas. Once we discern how a particular genre works, we will be ready to ask more effectively the six key questions of biblical exploration.

Review Questions

Write *T* in the blank if the statement accurately reflects the content of this chapter and *F* if it does not.

_____1. The goal of biblical exploration (exegesis) is to understand the text as the original audience should have understood it or as the author did.

_____2. Considering genre when exploring the meaning of a passage is critical because the genre profoundly affects how we will ask the six questions of exploration.

Choose the answer that best represents the content of this chapter.

_____3. Melissa's chief mistake was

A. that she expected God to speak to her through His Word.

B. her failure to consider that Isaiah was written seven hundred years before Christ.

C. that she skipped exegesis.

D. not getting married earlier.

_____4. As we read the Scriptures, we broaden our circle of knowledge primarily by

A. diligently consulting commentaries and other good helps.

B. asking the right questions of the text.

C. waiting for spiritual insight.

D. reading the entire biblical book in one sitting.

5. Summarize in your own words Moses Stuart's significant observations.

6. What are the "right questions" to ask in biblical exploration?

7. "Explore" Galatians 2:20 by using the six questions introduced in this lesson. Although in the future you will be asked to consult other sources, for now limit your investigation to the text itself and its surrounding context.

8. Try using the six exploration questions for investigating Exodus 33:14.

CHAPTER THREE

Exploring the Epistles

3

Getting to Know the Epistles

For I am not ashamed of the gospel of Christ: for it is the power of God unto salvation to every one that believeth: to the Jew first, and also to the Greek. For therein is the righteousness of God revealed from faith to faith: as it is written, The just shall live by faith. (Rom. 1:16-17)

Moses my servant is dead; now therefore arise, go over this Jordan, thou, and all this people, unto the land which I do give to them, even to the children of Israel. (Josh. 1:2)

These two passages demonstrate how the New Testament epistles differ from other genres (in this case, biblical narrative). Unlike the historical books, the New Testament epistles are letters written to churches or individuals. Since they were written to believers involved in the same work that we are called to (the work of the church), they are more directly applicable to us today than any other type of biblical literature. While the verse from Joshua cannot be legitimately applied without knowing the rest of the story, the apostle Paul's famous affirmation, even if taken by itself, suggests its own applications.

Another distinguishing characteristic of these letters is their unusually dense doctrinal content. Though the epistles comprise only about ten percent of the Bible, they may contain just as much information on Bible doctrine as the remaining ninety percent. Joshua 1:2 gives us necessary information, laying the foundation for the rest of the story, but the verse contains no direct statement regarding any

KNOW the LETTERS

The epistles occupy a prominent place in the New Testament. Twenty-one of the twenty-seven New Testament books are letters. However, since these letters are considerably shorter than the other books, the epistles still comprise less than half of the New Testament text.

Romans	Titus
I and II Corinthians	Philemon
Galatians	Hebrews
Ephesians	James
Philippians	I and II Peter
Colossians	I, II, and III John
I and II Thessalonians	Jude
I and II Timothy	Revelation 2-3

biblical doctrine. Romans 1:16-17, however, introduces important information about God, Christ, salvation, the gospel, righteousness, and faith—each of which are key subjects in studies of Bible doctrine. If a believer lacks the skill necessary to understand this part of Scripture, he will have difficulty understanding the fundamental doctrines of his faith.

And don't kid yourself—skill is necessary to exegete the epistles. How hard can reading a letter be? Although the epistles are letters, they are written in a style like no letter we would ever write. Letters in the New Testament are grammatically complex—characterized by long sentences filled with participles, infinitives, and various subordinate clauses. This grammatical complexity is the greatest challenge to understanding the epistles. The devoted and responsible student of Scripture will take time to learn and appreciate that difficult style.

*E*xplore an Epistle

Remember that the key to successful exploration is asking the right questions about the text. But before you begin asking those questions, you need to get familiar with the text. So when you begin your study of an epistle, you should, first of all, read the letter several times, doing each reading in one sitting. During these preliminary readings, you should note the overall flow of thought. You will also need to mark words or phrases that you do not understand. To resolve such difficulties, look at several different

Think About It!

Why read the entire letter in one sitting? Most likely, the authors expected their correspondence to be read this way. Think about it. Imagine that you are a pastor in a difficult situation. Your mentor in the ministry has written you a six-page, divinely inspired letter to encourage you. Do you suppose that your mentor would expect you to read only one page per day until you were finished? Yet this is exactly how many people "study" I Timothy. If we want to understand the text, we should start by reading it the way it was meant to be read.

translations and see how they express those problematic words or phrases. If the translations prove unhelpful, hold your questions until later in the study.

Where, When, Who

Once you are familiar with the epistle, you can start asking the questions essential for effective exploring. *Where, when,* and *who* all concern *historical context.* This is the setting in history that has produced the need for the epistle. You must learn about the circumstances and people that stand behind the text before you can discern the full significance of the text itself.

Bible encyclopedias and the introductions in various commentaries will effectively familiarize you with the historical context. With most epistles, the key source for historical background is found in the Book of Acts. Therefore, as you investigate the commentaries and Bible encyclopedias, be sure you use the tools that guide you through the pertinent information found in Acts. You must also be careful not to *overuse* the commentaries at this point. After you have read the epistle several times, you will be tempted to start reading the main text of the commentary to see what the experts have to say about individual verses. However, you must control your curiosity or else it will spoil future rewards and hinder your present skill development.

GET THE BIG PICTURE

Introduction
  I. Historical Analysis—*Where, When, Who*
 II. Thematic Analysis—*What*
III. Purpose Analysis—*Why*
IV. Structural Analysis—*How*
Conclusion

Use these resources, first of all, to learn about the author and recipients of the epistle *(who)*. In your study journal, jot down information that is new and interesting to you. Second, read the sections that deal with the cultural setting and events surrounding the writing of the epistle *(where* and *when)*. Often this information will be presented in the sections dealing with the author and the recipients. Significant information on *where* and *when* will also be found in the sections labeled "Date," "Place," and "Occasion." Again, be sure to jot down potentially helpful information in your study journal so that you can refer to it later.

What Would You Say?

After reading some background information for Philippians, Ephesians, and I John, look up the following passages: Philippians 4:10-13, Ephesians 2:14-22, and I John 1:1-4. How does the historical background influence your understanding of each passage?

What

When you have noted some important facts about the historical context, you will be ready to observe the *what*—the *written context*. In this step you will be noting the themes or topics that the author develops in his letter.

Finding the Seams

First, you should carefully read through a spacious, unmarked copy of the epistle (perhaps a photocopy from a wide-margin Bible) and find the thematic divisions in the text. Wherever the author seems to be changing topics, draw a line to separate the end of one section from the beginning of another. When you finish, you should reexamine each section and label it with its main idea. Though this exercise is theoretically simple and straightforward, it will at times be frustrating. But be persistent, for—as with any skill—only practice will make you consistently effective.

Do not depend on the chapter divisions for this step. Though chapter divisions usually mark a logical change in the text, many do not (e.g., the breaks between II Cor. 1-2, II Cor. 4-5, and Eph. 4-5). The only way you will know whether a chapter division marks a new topic is by thinking through the text on your own. Furthermore, most epistles have several logical divisions within one chapter. So if you depend on the chapter breaks, you will miss many logical divisions.

After you have tentatively divided and labeled the text, you will need to check your analysis by looking at a study Bible. Such Bibles are usually thorough in their dividing and labeling of the text. Another good resource is a commentary. Most commentaries in their introductory pages give a detailed outline of the epistle they cover, indicating the verses that correspond to each part of the outline.

"So," perhaps you are thinking, "if study Bibles and commentaries have already found the 'seams' in the text, why should *we* bother?" A good question—for which there are two good answers. First, since these tools often do not agree, you must form your own opinions regarding the logic of the text before you can use these tools profitably. Second, what you earn will mean much more to you than what you are given. If you personally toil over the epistle's thought flow, you will appreciate that knowledge much more and remember it much better than if you simply memorized the same information from a commentary.

Ancient Greek manuscript showing portions of I John 4-5, illustrating the absence of chapter divisions.

THE GENERAL EPISTLE OF
JAMES

greeting

James, a servant of God and of the Lord Jesus Christ, to the twelve tribes which are scattered abroad, greeting.

rejoicing in temptations

2 My brethren, count it all joy when ye fall into divers temptations;
3 Knowing this, that the trying of your faith worketh patience.
4 But let patience have her perfect work, that ye may be perfect and entire, wanting nothing.

finding wisdom

5 If any of you lack wisdom, let him ask of God, that giveth to all men liberally, and upbraideth not; and it shall be given him.
6 But let him ask in faith, nothing wavering. For he that wavereth is like a wave of the sea driven with the wind and tossed.
7 For let not that man think that he shall receive any thing of the Lord.
8 A double minded man is unstable in all his ways.

union in the church

9 Let the brother of low degree rejoice in that he is exalted:
10 But the rich, in that he is made low: because as the flower of the grass he shall pass away.
11 For the sun is no sooner risen with a burning heat, but it withereth the grass, and the flower thereof falleth, and the grace of the fashion of it perisheth: so also shall the rich man fade away in his ways.

God's goodness in temptation

12 Blessed is the man that endureth temptation: for when he is tried, he shall receive the crown of life, which the Lord hath promised to them that love him.
13 Let no man say when he is tempted, I am tempted of God: for God cannot be tempted with evil, neither tempteth he any man:
14 But every man is tempted, when he is drawn away of his own lust, and enticed.
15 Then when lust hath conceived, it bringeth forth sin: and sin, when it is finished, bringeth forth death.
16 Do not err, my beloved brethren.
17 Every good gift and every perfect gift is from above, and cometh down from the Father of lights, with whom is no variableness, neither shadow of turning.
18 Of his own will begat he us with the word of truth, that we should be a kind of firstfruits of his creatures.

hearing the Word properly

19 Wherefore, my beloved brethren, let every man be swift to hear, slow to speak, slow to wrath:
20 For the wrath of man worketh not the righteousness of God.
21 Wherefore lay apart all filthiness and superfluity of naughtiness, and receive with meekness the engrafted word, which is able to save your souls.
22 But be ye doers of the word, and not hearers only, deceiving your own selves.
23 For if any be a hearer of the word, and not a doer, he is like unto a man beholding his natural face in a glass:
24 For he beholdeth himself, and goeth his way, and straightway forgetteth what manner of man he was.
25 But whoso looketh into the perfect law of liberty, and continueth therein, he being not a forgetful hearer, but a doer of the work, this man shall be blessed in his deed.

Stating the Theme

After you have identified the various sections in the book, examine your labels and try to express all the contents of the epistle in a one-sentence theme statement. Though you may be tempted to state this idea in more than one sentence, discipline yourself to express the book's content concisely. At the same time, however, you must make sure that your statement is broad enough to cover *all* the sections in the epistle. As you continue to study the epistle you will probably modify your theme statement somewhat.

Why

Asking *why* combines what you have learned about historical context and written context. In this step you must repeatedly ask yourself, "Given this historical setting, why did the author cover these themes with his audience?" You may be tempted to doubt the importance of this question. After all, if we thoroughly understand what the author said to his original audience, exegesis is complete, right? But that's a mighty big *if.* Investigating the author's purpose helps us double-check our conclusions. Furthermore, knowing *why* helps us to interrelate the *whats* as well as demonstrate which themes are the most important to the author's argument.

To get the *why* answered, you should go back through your copy of the epistle and label the reason that the author has included each section in his letter. Then you should compose a one-sentence purpose statement for the entire book. You will develop this general statement by combining all of your specific purpose labels. You may want to double-check your understanding of the epistle's purpose by seeing what the commentaries say on that subject. Often a commentator will discuss the letter's purpose in his introduction.

How

Determining how the author has expressed his ideas is the next step. This step allows you to double-check your analysis of the author's purpose and gives you a much better grasp of the epistle's themes, showing you how they fit together logically.

In this stage you will do what is called a **structural analysis.** Basically, a structural analysis is an outline of a book or paragraph that displays how each statement relates to the others. You should begin by searching through the first section of the epistle (after the greeting), looking for the first independent clause. A clause is a group of related words containing a subject and predicate. An independent clause is one that expresses a complete thought. Write out that clause in your study journal, placing the first word of the clause against the left margin. Under this independent clause list all the clauses and extended phrases that are grammatically dependent on it. Each of these should be indented from the left margin so that you can visualize their dependence on the independent clause. Any extended phrases or clauses that are dependent on other dependent expressions should be indented even farther. You should place each new independent clause at the left margin and begin the process again.

As you display the sections in this way, you will need to be looking for the thesis of each section. A thesis statement, or topic sentence, is the sentence that expresses what the section is about. Usually you can spot the thesis by noting which statement is logically independent of all the others. Such a clause should be labeled

• Structural analysis of James 1:2-4 •

thesis for section	a	My brethren, count it all joy
time of *a*	b	when ye fall into divers temptations;
cause of *a*	c	Knowing this,
content of *c*	d	that the trying of your faith worketh patience.
repetition of thesis	e	But let patience have her perfect work,
purpose of *e*	f	that ye may be perfect and entire,
description of *perfect*	g	wanting nothing.

"thesis for section." Once you have found the thesis, be sure to label the logical relationships between the lines. In order to label each line effectively, you will have to familiarize yourself with some of the most common logical relationships that occur between groups of words.

Common Logical Relationships

Time—An idea may be further developed by a statement of time. Usually chronological elements are introduced by words such as *while, when, during,* or *after.* Notice that the introductory clause in the following sentence gives more information about the timing of the main clause: "*When* we bring your names to the throne of grace, we give thanks to God for your spiritual growth." Often the idea of time can be communicated simply by a participle, which is a verb form functioning as an adjective and ending in *-ing, -ed,* or *-d* (e.g., *looking, having loved,* or *being concerned*). So the time idea in the previous example may be expressed in an epistle with a participial phrase: "*Bringing* your names to the throne of grace, we give thanks to God for your spiritual growth." However, be careful about labeling a participle as referring to an aspect of time. A participle can communicate a number of other logical relationships depending on the context.

Cause—Causal clauses reveal the reason a certain action has happened or the evidence indicating that a given statement is true. Cause is most commonly introduced by *because* or by a participle. Notice that the following two statements express the same meaning: "I started attending Faith Baptist Church *because* I knew the pastor was a good man"; "I started attending Faith Baptist Church, *knowing* the pastor was a good man." Another common way to introduce cause is the conjunction *for:* "Do not give in to the flesh, *for* the Lord will chasten all of His disobedient children."

Purpose—A purpose clause or phrase expresses the goal or intent of a previous statement. Usually it is introduced by the words *in order to, in order that, that,* or *to.* So, while witnessing, you may tell a person, "God sent His Son *to* die on the cross *that* you might live forever with Him." *To die on the cross* expresses the purpose of the clause *God sent His Son,* and *that you might live forever with Him* expresses the purpose of the phrase *to die on the cross.*

Result—A result clause or phrase represents the consequence of the clause it modifies. This consequence may be intended or unintended. Sometimes a result phrase is introduced by a participle, as in the following example. "The Pharisees were most concerned with maintaining their traditions, *ignoring* the Word of God." More often, however, the signal words *so that* or *so* introduce the idea. "Abraham believed the promises of God, *so* he became the father of many nations." Many times an author will connect two independent clauses (or even two paragraphs) by indicating that the second clause is the logical consequence of the first. In such situations the common signal words are *therefore* and *wherefore.* "Christ has paid the penalty for our sins completely. *Therefore,* let us not be discouraged about past failures."

Content—Another common relationship is content. Such a clause communicates the content of a statement, observation, or thought. Usually it is introduced by the word *that.* Note the following sentence: "God knows *that* all men need His salvation." In this quotation *that* introduces a content clause because the idea of all men needing salvation is the content of what God knows. Be careful not to confuse the content *that* with the purpose *that.* For example, in the sentence "God has made known His gospel to men *that* they might praise His name forever," *that* expresses purpose. Praising God forever is not the content of the gospel; it is God's purpose in declaring the gospel. Sometimes it is difficult to distinguish content from purpose. How would you label this one: "Paul prayed *that* his converts would come to know the Lord better"?

Description—An author may choose to develop an idea by employing some description. This is a phrase or clause that functions as an adjective. Consequently it will answer the question *which one, what kind, how many,* or *whose.* Usually this idea is expressed with a relative clause, a clause that begins with a relative pronoun *(who, whom, whose, which, that,* or *what)* and functions as an adjective. Notice the following two sentences: "He is the man *who* knows me well"; "He is the good man." The clause introduced by *who* tells us what kind of man this person is, as does the adjective *good.*

Concession—A concession clause admits a fact that would seem to contradict the statement it modifies. When an author inserts a concession, he is acknowledging that two apparently incompatible statements are true. Often such a clause is introduced by *though,* or *although.* There are, however, other ways to express the idea of concession. Note the following examples. "*Although* the Lord placed him in a perfect environment, Adam sinned and failed God." "Paul offered to pay Philemon for all the wrongs of Onesimus, *though* Philemon owed the apostle things far more valuable than Onesimus' service." "Jesus Christ, *being* God Himself, accepted the shameful death of the cross."

Manner/Means—Manner makes a sentence more colorful by describing how an action is performed. Means, on the other hand, tells the instrument by which an action is accomplished. Though these two relationships are logically distinct, they are easy to confuse. Each answers the question *how?* or *in what way?* and each is introduced by the same signal words: most often *with, by,* or just a participle. Here are some examples: "He opened the bottle *with* his teeth" (means); "He opened the bottle *with* vigor" (manner); "The rich young ruler departed from Christ, *sorrowing*" (manner); "Then the whole assembly was frightened *by* a loud clap of thunder" (means). For our purposes it is not necessary to distinguish between the two relations. It is sufficient to label something as simply *manner/means.*

Condition—A clause communicating a condition states a situation that must be met in order for the clause it modifies to be true or to happen. Usually the clause will be introduced by the word *if.* The following sentence reminds us of the condition that must be met before a person can be saved. "*If* you will repent and believe the gospel, God will forgive you of your sins." Sometimes students get confused about which clause modifies which. The independent clause in a conditional sentence is the second one. The *if* clause is grammatically dependent on the following clause.

Comparison—The author may choose to move from one thought to another by using a comparison; that is, he may advance his argument by stating that something mentioned previously is similar to something else. Often this is expressed by the combination *just as . . . so also.* In addition, the words *like* or *as* often introduce comparison. Note these two examples: "*Just as* Christ lived the life of a servant, *so also* Christians must not live for themselves"; "Welcome this new convert into your home, *as* you would your own child."

Contrast—Contrast is just the opposite of comparison. Often the author will set two things in opposition in order to emphasize their differences. A contrast is usually introduced by the conjunction *but*. The following sentence contrasts God's nature with man's: "Human beings may give their lives for someone they love dearly and deem to be good and righteous, *but* God gave His Son to die for sinners, His enemies."

Finishing the How

As you study these relationships, do not simply memorize the key words that introduce certain ideas. Instead, focus on understanding the *meaning* of each logical relationship. Though these introductory words are important and helpful, the epistles sometimes use other means to express these relationships.

When studying shorter epistles, this kind of detailed structural analysis is manageable. However, doing such a display of Romans would be a daunting task. When studying such epistles, you may want to display only those portions that are especially complex and difficult to understand. Nevertheless, working out a structural analysis of the entire epistle is still very helpful. This kind of study may take many weeks, but once you learn the grammatical complexities of a book, you can use that valuable information for the rest of your life.

Wrapping It Up

Before you record the results of this study, you may need to investigate the meaning of the text further. As you recall, while you are doing the preliminary readings, you should note any word or phrase that you do not understand and then see how other translations handle those difficulties. As you will soon discover, such a search will not answer all your questions. At this point (after you have asked your six questions), you should go back to those difficulties (and any difficulties you have uncovered since then) and see what the main text in the commentaries has to say about those words and phrases. Once you understand these difficult portions, record what you think is the correct interpretation in your study journal.

After you have "roughed in" your exploration, you will need to take all that you have learned about the text, condense it, and then preserve it in a safe place where you can easily access it in the future. The best place to preserve your conclusions is a wide-margin Bible.

To record your findings, first of all take your theme statement (which you've probably revised by now) and write it at the beginning of the epistle. Then write next to it the general purpose statement for the letter (which you've probably revised as well). Next you should draw in the section breaks throughout the epistle. Then you can place in the margin the summary statement you chose for each section and put the purpose statement for that section with your summary statement. With that done, go back through each section and underline at least the essence of each independent clause, which should highlight for you the grammatical backbone of the passage. Then, to remind yourself of each section's logical development, mark with a highlighter each key word introducing a dependent clause, lengthy phrase, or independent clause logically dependent on the thesis statement. Finally, wherever you have room in the margins, record briefly the interpretation of difficult statements in the text.

Once you finish your study, your Bible will contain, in distilled form, a clear record of what the text means. Though you will probably not refer to your more thorough notations often, do not discard them. Keep them in your study journal for ready reference. In time you will forget some of your observations, and the notes you place in your Bible may not be sufficient to jog your memory. In such cases you will need to consult your more detailed study notes.

As you work through other epistles, you'll be gathering quite a library of vital observations that will help you understand God's Word. Treasure this study and the conclusions it will yield. While much of human endeavor provides only the means to meet a person's physical needs and desires, laboring in the vineyard of God's Word yields a divine message that guides the soul safely through this life—leading at last to an eternal home.

Review Questions

True or False

Write *T* in the blank if the statement accurately reflects the content of this chapter and *F* if it does not.

_____ 1. The greatest challenge to understanding the epistles lies in their grammatical complexity.

_____ 2. Next to the four Gospels (Matthew, Mark, Luke, and John), the epistles contain more information used in outlines of Bible doctrine than any other part of Scripture.

_____ 3. The original recipients of the epistles probably took weeks to read through the inspired correspondence.

Short Answer

4. How does the historical background for Philippians influence our understanding of Philippians 4:10-13?

5. When using commentaries to investigate *where, when,* or *who,* what section of the commentary should you limit yourself to?

6. What is the key source of information for the historical background of most epistles?

Choose the logical relationship that each italicized clause or phrase expresses.

A.	cause	G.	description
B.	comparison	H.	manner
C.	concession	I.	means
D.	condition	J.	purpose
E.	content	K.	result
F.	contrast	L.	time

_____7. I will praise my God day and night, *who has blessed me with every kind of spiritual blessing.*

_____8. *Having loved us with an immeasurable love,* the Father sent His Son to die for our sins.

_____9. Brethren, I know *that God will soon release me from prison.*

_____10. When the apostles saw that God had ordained me to preach to the Gentiles, *as He had Peter to the Jews,* they detained me no longer.

_____11. *Although I cannot be with you in the flesh,* my spirit, through my prayers, communes with you.

_____12. When God called us to minister elsewhere, we left you in Ephesus, *rejoicing that God had worked in your hearts.*

_____13. *After Christ appeared to James,* all the apostles saw Him.

_____14. We give thanks to God for you, *making mention of you in our prayers.*

_____15. You turned away from idols *to serve the living and true God.*

_____16. You are not under the law, *but under grace.*

_____17. The Gentiles, *being ignorant of Moses and the prophets*, do still know the law of God, for it is written in their hearts.

_____18. You cannot receive the gospel *with your mind only.*

_____19. The rulers of this world did not know who Jesus was, *for if they had, they would not have crucified Him.*

_____20. The Judaizers preach their own version of the gospel *that they may trap you in their bondage.*

_____21. Jesus Christ was declared to be the Son of God *with power* when He was raised from the dead.

_____22. False teachers refuse to accept the truth about Christ, *and so they are condemned by God.*

Exercises

Turn to Ephesians 1-2 in your Bible and divide the text into sections, according to the various themes developed there.

23. What are the sections?

24. What titles did you assign to the various sections?

25. On your own paper, display a structural analysis of I Thessalonians 1.

*P*roject

Following the suggestions outlined in this chapter, explore the epistle that your teacher assigns.

CHAPTER FOUR

Exploring the Psalms

4

What Makes the Psalms Different?

The first time I thumbed through a modern version, I was surprised at what I saw in the Psalms. Each psalm was set off in poetic stanzas. "Wow!" I thought, "God must like poetry because one of the longest books in the Bible is simply an anthology of poems." But as I read farther, I soon came to a discovery of another kind. I was disappointed to find that the Psalms did not *sound* like poetry—even in a modern version. "Poems should rhyme and evidence an obvious sound pattern," I puzzled, "just like the poetry I've studied in school."

The Lord is my shepherd

> The Assyrian came down like a wolf on the fold,
> And his cohorts were gleaming in purple and gold;
> And the sheen of their spears was like stars on the sea,
> When the blue wave rolls nightly on deep Galilee.
>
> —from "The Destruction of Sennacherib" by George Gordon, Lord Byron

Unlike Byron's poetry, however, the Psalms I looked at seemed to move along aimlessly and showed not even the slightest hint of a rhyme scheme.

> The heavens are reporting the glory of God;
> And the sky is telling of the work of His hands.
> Day bubbles over to day with speech,

Since Psalms is the best loved and most read book of biblical poetry, this chapter will focus on that part of the Bible. However, biblical poetry extends far beyond the Psalms and includes works significantly different from the worship poetry found in the Psalms. The wisdom poetry of the Old Testament is recorded primarily in Job, Proverbs, Ecclesiastes, and the Song of Solomon. Proverbs is distinctive in that it is written as proverbial wisdom poetry. Most of the major and minor prophets evidence prophetic poetry. Poems of various kinds are also found sprinkled throughout the narratives of the Bible (e.g., Exod. 15:1-21; Judg. 14:14; I Sam. 2:1-10; Rev. 15:3-4).

And night announces knowledge to night.

—from Psalm 19 (author's rendering)

But at that point I was familiar with only a certain kind of poetry—rhymed poetry. I had assumed that rhyme (the distinguishing characteristic of only one kind of poetry) was the essence of all poetry. This flawed assumption became obvious to me when I remembered that some of the world's greatest poems do not rhyme. No one would seriously charge that Milton's *Paradise Lost* was not poetry, but as its first six lines prove, this epic comes no closer to rhyming than Psalm 19 does.

> Of man's first disobedience, and the fruit
> Of that forbidden tree whose mortal taste
> Brought death into the World, and all our woe,
> With loss of Eden, till one greater Man
> Restore us, and regain the blissful seat,
> Sing, Heavenly Muse . . .

So if rhyme is not the essential characteristic of poetry, what is it that makes poetry *poetry?* Seeking an answer to that question was for me the first step in a very important journey—one that led to a much deeper appreciation for the beauty and power of biblical poetry.

GET THE BIG PICTURE

Orientation: What is Poetry?
Multilevel Parallelism
Figurative Expression
I. Setting Analysis—*Where, When, Who*
II. Poetic Analysis—*How*
III. Thematic Analysis—*What*
IV. Purpose Analysis—*Why*

Multilevel Parallelism

Poetry distinguishes itself from prose as a more powerful and beautiful expression of thought. The poet creates this sense of exalted communication through extensive use of multilevel parallelism and figurative expression. Unlike other genres, poetry repeats sounds and ideas at regular intervals. For English speakers this parallelism is primarily parallelism of sound. This includes the rhyme scheme (parallelism between lines), the metrical pattern (a parallelism within a line), and the stanza form (parallelism between stanzas). Hebrew poetry, however, exhibits primarily parallelism of thought. Notice again our examples from Byron and Psalm 19.

> The Assyrian came down like a wolf on the fold,
> And his cohorts were gleaming in purple and gold;

> The heavens are reporting the glory of God;
> And the sky is telling of the work of His hands.

Byron's opening lines form a couplet with a clear rhyme and metrical pattern. The first verse from Psalm 19 also evidences parallelism. The *meaning* of the first line "rhymes" with the meaning of the second line. Both are communicating the same message but in different words: "the starry host constantly testifies to the fact that God is the Creator." Learning to sense this parallelism of thought is just as important for appreciating the Psalms as noticing the rhyme scheme is for enjoying English poetry.

Synonymous Parallelism

The most common form of Hebrew "thought rhyme" is *synonymous parallelism,* which repeats or restates in the following line what has been said in the preceding line.

> I will praise thee, O Lord, with
>   my whole heart;
> I will shew forth all thy
>   marvellous works.

> —Psalm 9:1

What Would You Say?

The omniscient, all-wise God has a good reason for everything He does, though at this time we may not perceive those reasons. Sometimes, however, there is sufficient evidence to give us a pretty good idea of why God has chosen a particular course of action. Can you think of a possible reason that God chose to record His poetry in parallelisms of meaning rather than sound?

51

Recognizing this kind of parallelism is an important part of interpretation primarily because it can help you understand general or obscure statements in a psalm. Note the following string of synonymous poetic lines.

> But the mercy of the Lord is from everlasting to
> everlasting upon them that that fear him,
> And his righteousness unto children's children;
> To such as keep His covenant,
> And to those who remember his commandments to do
> them.
>
> —Psalm 103:17-18

Can You Hear the "Rhyme"?

At first, "thought rhyme" may seem to lack the beautiful sound that English poems have. However, after you read a number of poems with this kind of parallelism, you begin to sense the beauty of this poetry—even in its sound. Take Psalm 114 as an example.

If you are not sure what exactly "fear Him" means in the first line, the synonymous parallelism proves informative. Those who fear the Lord are the same as those that "keep his covenant" and those that "remember his commandments to do them." Therefore, we learn from synonymous parallelism that a person who fears God is a person who obeys God.

Antithetical Parallelism

With *antithetical parallelism* the author states the opposite of a previous line in a following line. This type is found most frequently in the Book of Proverbs, though it is common in Psalms also.

> A soft answer turneth away wrath:
> But grievous words stir up anger.
>
> —Prov. 15:1

Relating the two antithetical lines to each other is often enlightening for interpretation. For example, Proverbs 10:12 states, "Hatred stirreth up strifes: / but love covereth all sins." If you interpret the second line by itself, you could come to some very odd and dangerous conclusions. You must remember, however, that this proverb is contrasting stirring something up (fire imagery) with covering something (its opposite—smothering imagery). Thus the verse does not teach that love ignores sin or renders failure inconsequential. Rather, the proverb asserts that while hatred ignites the flames of strife, the virtue of love, by showing kindness, smothers the glowing embers of potential sin—just as Proverbs 15:1 states.

Synthetic Parallelism

A third common category is *synthetic parallelism*. With this form the poet simply advances the thought of a previous line in a subsequent line.

> Enter not into judgment with thy servant:
> For in thy sight shall no man living be justified.
>
> —Psalm 143:2

Admittedly this is not really parallelism at all. *No man being justified* is not a repetition of *not entering into judgment,* nor is it the opposite. The second line (in this example, by expressing the cause or grounds of the first) simply further develops the previous line's thought. However, it is still a common aspect of Hebrew poetry, functioning as a "monotony breaker." The Hebrew author needed to avoid too much parallelism, which makes any poetry sound trite. By employing synthetic "parallelism," he could keep his work free from such an excess.

Emblematic Parallelism

The biblical poet often employs *emblematic parallelism* to make a comparison. The author states an image (an emblem) in the first line and in the second expresses the subject in reality. The words commonly used in this construction are *as . . . so.* Thus in the following example a thirsty deer becomes an emblem of a person who longs to know God.

> *As* the hart panteth after the water brooks,
> *So* panteth my soul after thee, O God.
>
> —Psalm 42:1

Climactic Parallelism

Climactic parallelism is a particular kind of synonymous parallelism in which the author begins a subsequent line of poetry with the exact words that began a previous line. In so doing, as the name suggests, the poet creates a sense of growing intensity, as the expression moves toward a climax.

> Give unto the Lord, O ye mighty,
> Give unto the Lord glory and strength.
> Give unto the Lord the glory due unto his name;
> Worship the Lord in the beauty of holiness.
>
> —Psalm 29:1-2

Figurative Expression

"Bryan!" I knew I was in trouble. Carl was a hard worker and a fair Christian boss, but a good Bible interpreter he was not. As I followed his voice, I somehow sensed that I was in for one of those unhappy "Bible discussions."

"How long do you think the week of Creation lasted?" Carl asked, his eyes betraying that he had already made up his mind. "Well," I began, "Genesis 1 uses the word *day,* so I think each day was a day. That means the week was just a week." "But isn't it true that 'a day is with the Lord as a thousand years and a thousand years as a day'?" Carl fired back. "The Bible does say that," I returned, "but the verse you just quoted is from a psalm, which is poetry. Poems are characterized by much figurative language. The language in narratives, however, is usually more literal. Since Genesis 1 is a narrative, we should expect *day* to refer to twenty-four hours." Carl, however, was not satisfied. "Stop playing with the text! It says 'a thousand years is as a *day.*'" "Yes, the psalmist makes that comparison," I acknowledged, "but *Genesis 1* just says '*DAY*'!" From there our conversation deteriorated.

That day I found myself frustrated because Carl had forced me to argue for something that I knew was indisputable among those that understand how language works. What Carl refused to admit under the pressure of an argument, people in general know to be true from experience. *Poetry differs from prose in the way it uses imagery.* Though figures of speech are found in all genres, they dominate poetry.

Figurative expression is the intentionally irregular and artful use of words or syntax that the author employs to accomplish mainly two effects. First, such language functions to heighten the emotional impact of a poem. By comparing various elements in the poem to other things or persons, the poet exalts his message above other forms of expression. Second, poets use such imaginative wording to slow down the reader. By complicating the communication with images and difficult allusions, the poet forces the reader to work with the text. In the process of unraveling the communication, the reader comes to appreciate the significance of the poet's message.

> *Figurative expression is the intentionally irregular and artful use of words or syntax.*

Note the different effects the following poems produce. Which one do you think is "better poetry"?

> Methought I saw my late espouséd saint
> Brought to me like Alcestis from the grave,
> Whom Jove's great son to her glad husband gave,
> Rescued from death by force though pale and faint.
> Mine, as whom washed from spot of childbed taint,
> Purification in the old law did save,
> And such, as yet once more I trust to have
> Full sight of her in Heaven without restraint,
> Came vested all in white, pure as her mind.
> Her face was veiled, yet to my fancied sight,
> Love, sweetness, goodness, in her person shined
> So clear, as in no face with more delight.
> But O, as to embrace me she inclined,
> I waked, she fled, and day brought back my night.
>
> > —John Milton, "Methought I Saw My Late Espouséd Saint"
>
> Last night I dreamed that I did see my wife,
> Who seemed, though dead, alive and full of love.

She came to me all dressed in white—pure life
She lived—pure cloth her wrap, her robe above.
Then op't her arms to loose from me my strife.
But dream did end; she fled; my joy did move.

—Bryan Smith, "A Mangled Milton"

Though both have consistent rhyme and meter (multilevel parallelism), the second poem lacks figurative expression. Consequently, it is flat and reads unremarkably, like a rhymed report in a newspaper. Milton's work, however, gives the imagination much food for thought through its many figures and allusions. Milton also draws the reader to study his message by his difficult descriptions.

Like any serious reader of Milton, the responsible student of Scripture must familiarize himself with the mechanics of poetic figures of speech. The following paragraphs outline some of the more common figures of speech that occur in Psalms.

Analogical Expression

The most common poetic figures are forms of **analogical expression**—creative comparisons drawn between abstract ideas and concrete objects. Each figure in this category expresses an idea by stating one thing in terms of another.

One of the most common figures of speech, and certainly the easiest to recognize, is the **simile.** This is simply a comparison using the words *like* or *as.* So when the psalmist declares that the Messiah will defeat evildoers, he emphasizes his point with a

GET THE BIG
PICTURE

Types of Figurative Expression

The major figures of speech found in the Psalms can be categorized under three headings.

I. Analogical Expression   II. Allusion
    Simile   III. Irony
    Analogy   Simple Irony
    Metaphor   Hyperbole
    Conceit   Understatement
    Metonymy
    Synecdoche
    Personification
    Apostrophe

simile, "Thou shalt dash them in pieces <u>like</u> a potter's vessel" (Ps. 2:9). Sometimes a simile becomes more involved and develops into an **analogy,** which is an extended simile. Note how David's simile becomes an analogy in Psalm 55:6-8.

> And I said, Oh that I had wings <u>like</u> a dove!
> For then would I fly away, and be at rest.
> Lo, then would I wander far off,
> And remain in the wilderness. Selah.
> I would hasten my escape
> From the windy storm and tempest.

Perhaps the most frequently used analogical expression is the **metaphor.** A metaphor makes a comparison without using any comparative words. Metaphors express a comparison more powerfully than similes because they describe the subject as *actually being* the image. In Psalm 108:9, God scorns, "Moab is my <u>washpot</u>," degrading the country of Moab for its long enmity against God. Similarly, the Messiah, by using a metaphor, graphically highlights the vicious strength of His persecutors in Psalm 22:12, "Many <u>bulls</u> have compassed me: / strong <u>bulls</u> of Bashan have beset me round." As he may with a simile, the poet sometimes chooses to extend a metaphor over several sentences or more. An extended metaphor is called a **conceit.** The most famous conceit in the Psalms is David's use of *shepherd* in Psalm 23:1-4.

As you interpret similes and metaphors, you must correctly identify a very important three-part relationship. Both of these figures of speech involve a **tenor** (the subject in reality), a **vehicle** (the thing the subject is being compared to), and a **point of similarity.** Perhaps you have heard a frustrated parent (certainly not your own) exclaim, "These kids are pigs!" This familiar metaphor clearly states a tenor (kids) and a vehicle (pigs). To understand the statement, however, the listener must interpret the point of similarity between

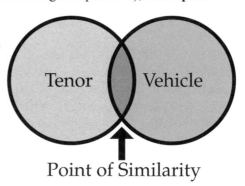

Point of Similarity

children and *pigs*. Could it be that they both *oink* and root around in the mud with their snouts? In most cases, at least, there is only one characteristic they share that is significant to the statement—both are messy. Consequently, the meaning of the statement is essentially, "These kids are messy." The metaphor, however, makes the communication more impressive.

Two mistakes are especially common when interpreting similes and metaphors. First, people tend to assume that the point of similarity is broader than the author intended. As was the case with the pig metaphor, often the point of similarity amounts to only one characteristic. Another common mistake is misinterpreting the significance of the point of similarity. If you are not familiar with the author's vehicle, you will not be able to appreciate the reason he chose that metaphor or simile, and thus the poem's powerful language will be lost to you, sounding simply "odd." "The hill of God is as the hill of Bashan" seems like a strange way to describe Mount Zion (Ps. 68:15). However, a little study in a Bible encyclopedia and atlas will not only reveal what most likely is the point of similarity in this simile, but it will also help the interpreter to see the poem as the poet did—a thing of beauty as well as a message.

"Well, Marge, if I don't hang up and check on Johnny, he'll start feeling like a caged bird."

Occasionally the point of similarity is quite broad—but rare.

Metonymy is another favorite figure of speech for the psalmists. This form of expression substitutes a thing somehow related (called a *metonym*) to the subject under consideration for the actual subject. The nature of the relationship between the metonym and the subject can differ greatly. Sometimes an author will use a physical object associated with a certain action to represent the action, as in Psalm 120:2, "Deliver my soul, O Lord, from <u>lying lips</u>, / and from a <u>deceitful tongue</u>." The poet is not asking to be preserved from actual lips or a physical tongue; he is asking the Lord to preserve him from lying—an action associated with one's lips and tongue. On the other hand, the psalmist may state the effect of a particular action when intending the action itself (called *effect-cause metonymy*): "Make me to hear <u>joy</u> and <u>gladness</u>; / that the bones which thou hast broken may rejoice" (Ps. 51:8). Most likely the metonyms *joy* and *gladness* refer to David's future rejoicing. This joy could result from only one action—God's forgiveness. Therefore, in plain language, David requests, "Let me hear you say, 'You are forgiven.'"

Synecdoche substitutes a part of a thing for the entire thing (often described as *part for the whole*). The second line of Psalm 51:8 contains synecdoche, "Make me to hear joy and gladness; / that the <u>bones</u> which thou hast broken may rejoice." David's bones are not the only things that he longs to see rejoice; he is asking God to give his entire being joy.

Be careful not to confuse metaphor, metonymy, and synecdoche. With a metaphor the author usually employs a vehicle that is not related to the tenor (e.g., "It was obvious that the man was in the <u>autumn</u> of his life"). Metonymy and synecdoche, however, use vehicles naturally related to their tenors. The vehicle in metonymy is usually an emblematic attribute of the tenor (e.g., "The <u>crown</u> of England no longer wields the authority it once did"). The vehicle in synecdoche, on the other hand, is actually part of the tenor, usually a member so conspicuous that the reader easily thinks of the entire tenor (e.g., "Children should be taught to respect the <u>hoary head</u>").

An author may also express a comparison by using **personification.** This figure makes the communication more vivid and forceful by attributing human qualities or actions to inanimate objects or ideas. Note Psalm 93:3, "the floods have lifted up, O Lord, / the floods have lifted up their voice; / the floods lift up their waves." A similar analogical expression is the **apostrophe,** by which the poet addresses inanimate objects (or persons not present) as though they could respond. While reviewing Israel's history, the psalmist employs this figure in proclaiming the greatness of God's deliverance: "What ailed thee, O thou sea, that thou fleddest? / thou Jordan, that thou wast driven back?" (Ps. 114:5).

Allusion

The psalms are rich with **allusions,** references within a poem (or any work of literature) to things outside it. Though the referent of any allusion will be external to the psalm, it will almost always belong to some part of Scripture. This figure of speech was a significant tool for biblical poets. Allusions allowed them to infuse their work with powerful emotional effects in just a few words. The feelings or convictions that took years to develop in Israel's history could be expressed in a psalm by a quick and simple allusion. Allusions also challenge the reader to slow down and study the psalm's message. If the reader wishes to enjoy the allusion and profit from it fully, he will have to do his homework. For example, try to identify the allusion in the following lines and see if you can determine its significance.

> Purge me with hyssop, and I shall be clean:
> Wash me, and I shall be whiter than snow.
>
> —Psalm 51:7

What Would You Say?

Allusions are common in the hymns you sing every week. Consider the hymn "Guide Me, O Thou Great Jehovah." Of this poem's eighteen lines, nine contain clear allusions to a particular part of the Bible. Can you identify the biblical allusions in the text of this hymn? How does recognizing those allusions affect your understanding and enjoyment of that hymn?

Irony

The word *irony* describes a class of figurative expressions that states one idea on the surface but conveys a different meaning below the surface. An author employs **simple irony** when his meaning is the opposite of the words he chooses. So Solomon ironically attacks materialism in Ecclesiastes 10:19: "A feast is made for laughter, / and wine maketh merry: / but money answereth [is the answer for] all these." Direct opposition is not the only way that words can convey a different meaning below the surface. The author's intent may differ from his wording in degree. Thus, irony can be accomplished through **hyperbole.** This figure is a purposeful overstatement that emphasizes a truth. David writes in Psalm 6:6, "All the night make I my bed to <u>swim</u>; / I <u>water</u> my couch with my tears." His bed is not actually floating in tear water; he simply means that he is overcome with sorrow. Irony can also be accomplished through the opposite of hyperbole, **understatement.** So when David confesses, "A broken and a contrite heart, O God, thou <u>wilt not despise</u>" (Ps. 51:17), he is understating the fact that God *delights* in contrition (cf. Ps. 10:17; 34:18).

Explore a Psalm

The psalms exhibit a subtle beauty and power that often evade the reader during his first few encounters with the text. Therefore, before you start asking the questions of biblical exploration, you will need to read the psalm at least three times. This exercise will be much more profitable if you use a version that sets off the text in poetic stanzas. To facilitate taking many notes, make a large photocopy of the psalm. After you have read the text several times, note words or expressions you do not understand and see how other translations express them. Once you have a general grasp of the poem's contents, you are ready to ask the familiar questions.

Where, When, Who

Asking *where, when,* and *who* is a bit more complicated in the Psalms because the psalmists, unlike the authors of the epistles, usually do not communicate directly with the reader. In a psalm the author teaches the reader by creating a setting, often giving voice to several different speakers and usually addressing God rather than the reader. For this reason the interpreter must investigate more than just the historical background of the psalm when he considers *where-when-who.* He must also study the setting and characters within the poem.

External Where, When, Who

If you have taken a literature course, you know that textbooks analyzing poetry are concerned with more than just the poems themselves. The editors usually divide the poetry into historical periods (Neoclassical, Romantic, Modern, and so forth). Each period begins with several pages discussing the significant events in that time span. Then the editors present the poems with a discussion of each poet's personal history.

What literature books in general recognize about poetry, the student of Scripture must also recognize about the psalms. Often the full impact of a psalm cannot be appreciated without knowing the circumstances that stand behind it. Consider Psalm 84:10—"A day in thy courts is better than a thousand. / I had rather be a doorkeeper in the house of my God, / than to dwell in the tents of wickedness." These words are much more meaningful once you realize that the "sons of Korah" were to sing this psalm. As this example indicates, a key source for this type of information is a psalm's title. These brief introductions usually indentify the author and often reveal helpful historical information.

To benefit fully from these titles, however, you will have to investigate the historical situation they refer to. For example, if you are studying Psalm 84, it is not enough simply to observe the title: "A Psalm for the sons of Korah." You must also check the cross-references and comments in a study Bible or commentary to learn what the title refers to. In this case you would discover that you needed to read Numbers 16, which records what happened to Korah—the namesake of the people in the title. While reading the chapter, you would jot down a summary of the background information in your study journal. Only by learning who the major characters are, where the events took place, and when the events happened would you be able to approach the psalm with the understanding that the author expects his readers to possess.

Internal Where, When, Who

The most important kind of *where-when-who* information comes from the psalm itself. For those psalms that have no titles, it is the only *where-when-who* available. Such information concerns the psalm's atmosphere (or setting) and characters. As you read the psalm, identify the **locations** mentioned *(where),* using a Bible atlas if necessary. You should also check some commentaries to help you determine how those locations affect the psalm's interpretation. Then you should ponder the **mood** of the psalm *(when)*. Is the tone joyful, triumphant, or sad? If it is exuberant, what has caused the joy? If it seems desperate, what is the affliction? Asking such questions not only helps you interpret the themes of the poem *(what),* but it also opens your eyes to application possibilities. For example, if you are dealing with a guilty conscience, recognizing that the psalmist struggled with the same problem when he wrote Psalm 130 will prepare you to find rest for your soul.

You must also identify three important **classes of people** in each psalm *(who).* First, take note of the psalm's *speakers.* Often the speaker will change with little or no indication. To notice such changes, you will have to pay close attention to shifts in perspective. Noting the change from one speaker to another can help indicate the structure and themes of a psalm. Second, mark the persons *spoken to* in the psalm. Most often, the person being addressed will be either God or fellow believers. Statements made to the Lord will differ in their significance from those spoken to one's contemporaries. Finally, in order to grasp the significance of each statement, you will need to identify those *spoken about* in the psalm.

What Would You Say?

Read Psalm 2. Note the changes in speakers throughout the psalm by using the guidelines discussed in this chapter. How does noting these changes in perspective help in analyzing the themes of this psalm? Can you develop an outline for Psalm 2 based on your observations of its speakers?

The Messianic Psalms

For centuries scholars have recognized thirteen psalms as uniquely or partially messianic.

Messiah Spoken About—8, 72, 89, 109, and 132

Messiah Spoken To—45, 102, and 110

Messiah Himself Speaks—2, 16, 22, 40, and 69

Nowhere does asking *who* become more significant than in dealing with **messianic psalms.** These are psalms in which the Messiah Himself speaks or is discussed. Some of these are *uniquely messianic;* that is, every word concerns the Messiah. Other psalms, however, are *partially messianic.*

Think About It!

Sometimes statements within partially messianic psalms express two different meanings—one concerning the psalmist and the other referring to the Messiah. In such psalms it appears that not even the psalmist was aware his poem contained messianic predictions. Is it possible that a poem can express two legitimate meanings and still make sense? When dealing with this interpretive difficulty, you must remember that the Bible is a divine and human book. Since the Scripture has two authors, there are places where the text communicates two different meanings (e.g., Ps. 69:9; John 2:17; Rom. 15:3). Though the psalmists wrote under inspiration, there were times when they did not fully understand the text they wrote (I Pet. 1:10-12). Because of the nature of the Scripture, such double meanings are not troubling. We should be thankful for the insight the Lord has given us in the New Testament, and we should use that advanced revelation to understand the Psalms more fully.

How can you tell which statements refer to the Messiah in such psalms? Two observations are especially helpful in this regard. First, a statement or description that, because of its loftiness, cannot refer to any finite, sinful creature should be taken as a reference to Christ (e.g., Ps. 40:7-8). Second, a statement that the New Testament attributes to the Messiah must, of course, be interpreted in the same way (cf. Ps. 69:9; Rom. 15:3). As you finish this part of your exegesis, be sure that you have recorded your significant *where-when-who* findings in your study journal.

How

Since the manner in which the poet has stated his message is essential for understanding a poem, you should consider the psalmist's figures of speech and parallelisms before investigating the psalm's *what*. With your photocopy before you, read through the psalm again and circle every figure of speech you encounter, label each one, and briefly state the effect that you think each figure has on the psalm. Remember that understanding the significance of certain figurative expressions requires further investigation. Seek the help of commentaries, Bible encyclopedias, and Bible atlases if necessary. Next, note the parallelism of the psalm.

KJV of Psalm 19:1-6 in poetic lines with parallelism and figures of speech noted:

Synonymous ⎡The heavens <u>declare</u> the glory of God;
⎣And the firmament <u>sheweth</u> his handywork. *personification*

Synonymous ⎡Day unto day <u>uttereth</u> speech,
⎣And night unto night <u>sheweth</u> knowledge.

Synthetic ⎡There is no speech nor language,
⎣Where their <u>voice</u> is not heard.

Synonymous ⎡Their line is gone out through all the earth,
⎣And their words to the end of the world.

Synthetic ⎡In them hath he set a **tabernacle** for the sun, *metaphor*
⎣Which is *as a bridegroom* coming out of his chamber, *simile*

Synthetic ⎡And rejoiceth *as a strong man* to run a race.
⎣His going forth is from the end of the heaven,

Synthetic ⎡And his circuit unto the ends of it:
⎣And there is nothing hid from the heat thereof.

Label the relationships between the lines and try to comment on the significance of each occurrence of parallelism.

What

In an epistle the author usually covers his themes in a linear fashion. He develops all of a given theme in one section before moving on to the next idea; thus, the logic moves forward in a straight line. The Hebrew poets, on the other hand, express their thoughts with powerful emotion and usually follow a cyclical, or repetitive, structure. Though this pattern may seem like a frustrating way to teach such important lessons, you must remember that a poem is not a

ROMANS

PROMISES TO ISRAEL	CH. 9–11
SANCTIFICATION	CH. 6–8
JUSTIFICATION	CH. 4–5
GUILT	CH. 1–3

lecture or sermon. It is an emotional work of art. Like a symphony, the psalm guides the reader through a series of recurring themes as it moves toward a climax and resolution.

Because of the cyclical nature of Hebrew poetry, you must ask the *what* differently than you did with the epistles. Rather than looking for the sections of the poem, you will need to discern the various *recurring themes*. You may find it helpful to trace these themes through the poem with colored pencils. After you have read the psalm several times, you will probably be familiar with the major

Themes	Psalm 63		Verses
JUDGMENT of the WICKED		9-10	11b
DEPENDENCE on GOD		6-8	
PRAISE to GOD	3-4	5b	11a
DESIRE for FELLOWSHIP	1-2	5a	

themes. With those themes in mind, go back through the photocopy, highlighting each word or phrase that applies to a specific color/theme. Once you have color-coded the themes, you may still have several verses that are not colored. Ask yourself, "Do any of these statements logically belong to one of my existing categories?" If they do not, create a new category, or categories, that will include these statements. With the entire poem thus categorized, read through each theme (color) by itself and note how the author develops each theme. Then develop an outline of these topics in your study journal. Once you have identified the various themes, think about how they logically fit together in the psalm. Then develop a one-sentence theme statement for the entire psalm.

By following this strategy, you will convert the cyclical structure of the poem into a linear format. Some may object to this method, fearing that it destroys the beauty of the psalm. After all, if God wanted the text to be cyclical, why try to make it linear? Perhaps the best way to answer such an objection is for us to consider the following analogy. Analyzing a psalm is similar to studying a rose. To understand the structure and function of a rose, you have to pluck the flower to pieces. In such an analysis, the flower ceases to be a thing of beauty, but the student learns a

KJV of Psalm 63 in poetic lines with themes identified

O God, thou art my God; early will I seek thee:
My soul thirsteth for thee, my flesh longeth for thee
In a dry and thirsty land, where no water is;
To see thy power and thy glory,
So as I have seen thee in the sanctuary.
Because thy lovingkindness is better than life,
My lips shall praise thee.
Thus will I bless thee while I live:
I will lift up my hands in thy name.
My soul shall be satisfied as with marrow and fatness;
And my mouth shall praise thee with joyful lips:
When I remember thee upon my bed,
And meditate on thee in the night watches.
Because thou hast been my help,
Therefore in the shadow of thy wings will I rejoice.
My soul followeth hard after thee:
Thy right hand upholdeth me.
But those that seek my soul, to destroy it,
Shall go into the lower parts of the earth.
They shall fall by the sword:
They shall be a portion for foxes.
But the king shall rejoice in God;
Every one that sweareth by him shall glory:
But the mouth of them that speak lies shall be stopped.

KEY:
Desire for fellowship with God
Praise to God
Dependence on God
Judgment of the wicked

---

great deal through the process. Unlike a rose, however, the psalm can be reassembled. After you have analyzed it by listing and developing the themes, you are then able to *experience* the psalm and thus have the best of both worlds. You can experience the psalm's circling emotion—by reading or singing it (if you have a copy of the Psalms set to music)—and benefit from a thorough understanding of the poet's message.

Some Hebrew poems evidence a linear structure. You should study such poems as you did the epistles. Read the psalm looking for the logical divisions in the text. Mark those divisions and then label them according to their contents. Then analyze the development of the sections by outlining each.

Before you finish this step, you will need to take care of some unfinished business. At this point you will probably still have some unresolved questions regarding the interpretation of certain words or phrases. Take some time to search some commentaries and find answers to those questions. Then record the answers in your study journal if you think that you will not be able to remember them.

Why

You can now effectively address why the poet has written the psalm. Did he want to convince the reader of something (to persuade)? Was he asking God for help (to supplicate)? Did he intend to inform the reader of something he had discovered about God (to inform/to praise)? Primarily by combining what you have learned from *where-when-who* and *what,* you can formulate a one-sentence statement expressing the psalmist's purpose in writing the poem.

DID YOU KNOW?

Example Purpose Statements

Psalm 4—To rebuke enemies and to express confidence in the Lord

Psalm 23—To testify to God's good guidance and to praise Him for His kind favor

Psalm 45—To praise the divine bridegroom and to exhort the bride to honor her husband

Psalm 51—To find spiritual restoration with God

Asking *why* can help you regain a proper focus on the psalm. After all this study, your mind may become a bit "cloudy." This step will help you recapture what the psalm is all about. It will also prepare you to enter the application phase, because knowing why the author wrote a psalm leads to understanding how it should affect your life.

Finalizing

As you finish your exegesis of the psalm, you should take some time to preserve the fruits of your labor. Make sure you have recorded in your study journal the significant observations you made while making your explorations. File your note-filled photocopy of the psalm in a safe place and record your basic conclusions in your wide-margin Bible. Briefly note in the margin the overall atmosphere of the psalm and mark the especially difficult figures of speech, giving a brief explanation in the margin. Then mark the most significant parallelisms and note their significance in the margin. Be sure to list the themes developed in the psalm, as well as the sentence stating the overall theme. If the poem has a linear structure, divide it into sections, just as you would a biblical letter. Finally, include your purpose statement at the beginning of the psalm.

Review Questions

Write *T* in the blank if the statement accurately reflects the content of this chapter and *F* if it does not.

_____1. Though not initially apparent, synthetic parallelism is a kind of Hebrew parallelism in the same sense that synonymous parallelism is.

_____2. An extended metaphor is called an *analogy*.

_____3. "Guide Me, O Thou Great Jehovah" is filled with examples of *allusion*.

_____4. All the psalms evidence a cyclical thematic structure.

Multiple Choice

Choose the answer that best represents the content of this chapter.

_____5. Hebrew poetry exhibits primarily what kind of parallelism?

  A. parallelism of sound
  B. parallelism of thought
  C. parallelism of stanza form

_____6. What is the major advantage of recognizing synonymous parallelism?

    A. It can clarify general or obscure statements in the psalm.

    B. It will keep you from misunderstanding the significance of the repetition of ideas.

    C. It will allow you to enjoy the beauty of the psalm.

    D. If you do not understand synonymous parallelism, you cannot understand any statement in a psalm.

_____7. The messianic psalms can be subdivided into

    A. absolutely messianic and relatively messianic psalms.

    B. uniquely messianic and partially messianic psalms.

    C. gently messianic and triumphantly messianic psalms.

    D. divinely messianic and humanly messianic psalms.

Short Answer

8. What makes poetry different from other genres?

9. Why do you think God chose not to express His poetic revelation in sound poetry?

10. What is *figurative expression,* and why do poets use it?

11. What is *analogical expression?*

12. What is the key source for information regarding a psalm's external *where-when-who?*

13. What are the key things to consider while investigating a psalm's internal *where-when-who?*

14. How can you tell that a statement refers to the Messiah?

15. Define the following terms: tenor, vehicle, point of similarity.

Identify the following examples of Hebrew parallelism.

      A. antithetical   D. synthetic
      B. climactic   E. synonymous
      C. emblematic

_____ 16. A father to the fatherless
Is the Lord God of hosts.

_____ 17. The wicked say, "The Lord will not hear."
But even those words, O God, You know.

_____ 18. Sing to the Lord, O kings of the earth;
Shout to Him a song of praise.

_____ 19. Save me, O God of Israel,
For my enemies seek my life.

_____ 20. As wax cannot withstand the fire,
So the wicked will fall in God's wrath.

_____ 21. God is our refuge and strength;
Our habitation, our fortress, our trust.

_____ 22. O God of hosts, hear our prayer;
O God of hosts, do not delay;
O God of hosts, remember our plight.

_____ 23. For Thy sake, O Lord, we are always in tribulation;
We are sent continually to slaughter.

_____ 24. O God, do not rebuke me in Your anger.
Remember mercy and forget Your wrath.

_____ 25. The upright will see the salvation of the Lord and be glad.
But the unrighteous will be ashamed.

Identify the following figures of speech.

     A. apostrophe   E. personification   I. allusion
     B. hyperbole   F. simile   J. understatement
     C. metaphor   G. synecdoche
     D. metonymy   H. simple irony

_____26. Old age is the winter of one's life.

_____27. O King David, I wish you were living at this time!

_____28. Save me, O Lord, for my enemies number more than the sand on the seashore.

_____29. The tongue of the wicked will not prosper.

_____30. If I had an eye like the eagle's, I could see no more clearly than I can by faith.

_____31. The floods of God's wrath cannot be held back forever.

_____32. Because of Adam's sin, God has called us all to sweat and tears.

_____33. The sea was stricken; it fled away in fear, for the Lord reigns.

_____34. As the lion roars over his prey, so the Lord will triumph in that day.

_____35. Rejoice, for the Lord's anointed will rule; he will hold the scepter.

Project

Following the suggestions outlined in this chapter, explore the psalm that your teacher assigns.

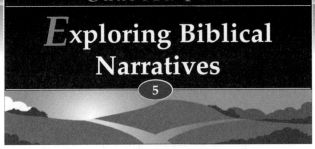

CHAPTER FIVE

Exploring Biblical Narratives

5

History Books or Storybooks?

"History is bunk"—at least Henry Ford thought so, and perhaps you do as well. But have you ever wondered *why* history books have such a bad reputation? Many students complain that the subject is just "boring." Names, wars, dates, dates, and more dates. Sometimes history books seem to comprise an aimless list of faceless people involved in tasks that exert no noticeable influence on life today. But if all history is unforgivably boring, we're in big trouble—because the Bible is primarily a book of history. Forty percent of the Old Testament and more than half of the New Testament record history. Furthermore, all Scripture fits together in a historical framework. The epistles, the Psalms, and the other genres all take place against the historical backdrop provided by the books of history.

However, before you roll your eyes and moan, you need to realize a key fact. Though the Bible is primarily history, it is not a history book but rather a series of *literary narratives*. Read the following paragraphs and see for yourself.

> During the reign of the succeeding pharaoh, Amenhotep IV (c. 1369-1353 B.C.), . . . the Empire went into sharp decline as the result of an internal struggle between the pharaoh and the powerful and wealthy priests of Amon.

GET THE BIG PICTURE

As the following list demonstrates, the Bible is primarily a book of history.

Genesis	Nehemiah
Exodus	Esther
Joshua	Job
Judges	Matthew
Ruth	Mark
I and II Samuel	Luke
I and II Kings	John
I and II Chronicles	Acts
Ezra	Revelation

The pharaoh undertook to revolutionize Egypt's religion by proclaiming the worship of the sun's disk, Aton, in place of Amon and all the other deities. Often called the first monotheist . . . Amenhotep changed his name to Akhenaton ("Devoted to Aton"), left Amon's city to found a new capital (Akhetaton), and concentrated upon religious reform. Most of Egypt's vassal princes in Asia defected when their appeals for aid against invaders went unheeded. Prominent among these invaders were groups of people called the Habiru, whose possible identification with the Hebrews of the Old Testament has interested modern scholars. . . . When Akhenaton died, his weak successor, Tutankhamen (c. 1352-1344 B.C.)—famed for his small but richly furnished tomb discovered in 1922—returned to Thebes and the worship of Amon.

—from T. Walter Wallbank's *Civilization Past & Present*, 22-23

And afterward Moses and Aaron went in, and told Pharaoh, Thus saith the Lord God of Israel, Let my people go, that they may hold a feast unto me in the wilderness. And Pharaoh said, Who is the Lord, that I should obey his voice to let Israel go? I know not the Lord, neither will I let Israel go. . . . Wherefore do ye, Moses and Aaron, let the people from their works? Get you unto your burdens. And Pharoah said, Behold, the people of the land now are many, and ye make them rest from their burdens. And Pharaoh commanded the same day the taskmasters of the people, and their officers, saying, Ye shall no more give the people straw to make brick, as heretofore: let them go and gather straw for themselves. . . . And Moses returned unto the Lord, and said, Lord, wherefore hast thou so evil entreated this people? Why is it that thou hast sent me? For since I came to Pharaoh to speak in thy name, he hath done evil to this people; neither hast thou delivered thy people at all. Then the Lord said unto Moses, Now shalt thou see what I will do to Pharaoh.

—Exodus 5:1–6:1

Though both excerpts concern the history of Egypt and the activities of a particular pharaoh, the style—and therefore the effect—of each is entirely different. Whereas the history book gives no dialogue, the biblical narrative presents hardly anything else. Although the secular historian does nothing to re-create a scene for the events he describes, the wording of the biblical narrative suggests a setting appropriate for the actions recorded. Furthermore, whereas the textbook historian discusses broad events and represents people impersonally, the Bible gives attention to individuals and describes their actions in great detail, carefully shaping and developing the main characters so that they come to life as we read the text. In short, history books recount history, but the Bible tells a story.

By choosing to write literary narratives rather than history books, the Lord records history in a way that is fun to read. If you have ever taught a children's Sunday school class, you know that it is rare to have a lesson on the Mosaic sacrificial system, Paul's explanation of original sin, or Daniel's description of the beast with ten horns. Usually the lessons are about biblical stories: Moses' crossing the Red Sea, David's defeating Goliath, or Jesus' healing of blind Bartimaeus. There are enough action, heroes, and villains in these narratives to keep even a fidgety four-year-old on the edge of his seat.

But God has given us these stories not simply to entertain us. He has chosen this genre primarily because it models the truths of Scripture by bringing them to life. Secular historians tell us what happened, but the biblical narratives *show* us what *happens*.

While reading these stories, we see that the struggles we face daily were common among the men and women that fill the biblical stage. We also learn that Jehovah is the God of history. He is intimately involved not only with the rise and fall of nations but also with the success or demise of every human being.

Knowing What to Expect

Good students are easy to spot. While others grumble about their unmanageable workload, stand-out students evidence an insatiable appetite for more. "What will we be covering next?" "Could I ask a few questions about next week's assignments?" "What will next year's courses be like?" Such students have learned an important lesson—knowing what to expect greatly enhances a person's ability to learn well. And just as a student can learn better if he knows what's coming next, so any reader of a biblical narrative can investigate the account more effectively if he knows what to look for in that narrative. We have already observed that the historical books are, in fact, stories, but now we must consider the three key elements that make those historical accounts stories. By getting familiar with these elements, you will learn what to look for as you investigate biblical narratives.

Plot

The stage lights dimmed, and we instinctively applauded. But when the house lights came up, I looked at my speech teacher and saw in his face the same disappointment I sensed was on my face. "Man, they needed to keep things *moving* in that play," I said,

---

GET THE BIG PICTURE

Introduction to Literary Narratives
- I. Plot
  - A. Conflict
  - B. Structure
- II. Character
  - A. Kinds of Characters
  - B. Methods of Revealing Characters
- III. Setting
  - A. Physical
  - B. Temporal
  - C. Cultural

reflecting on the boredom I had just experienced. Then my teacher made a perceptive comment, "The play was boring because it lacked conflict." And, as I later learned, since it lacked conflict, it also lacked plot, for the essence of plot is *structured conflict*. I left the performance hall that night with mixed emotions—satisfied that I knew why the play was not interesting, but irritated that I had wasted nearly two hours of my evening.

You may rest assured that you will never experience the same turmoil after reading the Scripture. Each biblical narrative evidences much conflict played out with careful structuring. This structure gives the stories an exciting sense of progression toward a goal. Because conflict and structure are so important to a narrative, we need to make sure we understand both concepts so that we can know what to look for in the plot of biblical stories.

Conflict

The most basic questions to ask of a narrative concern its conflict, for at the heart of every story is a battle. The nature of the opponents and their motives will vary, but in each case there will be war. Often a story's conflict can be described as **man against man,** one human character struggling against another. Sometimes, however, the conflict is subtler and involves the main character struggling with himself, usually called **man against himself.** Because the Bible is a divine book, we have abundant examples of conflicts that involve supernatural beings—**man against a greater power** or **a greater power against man.** The "greater power" is not always a person, however. It could be certain forces in nature or a difficult set of circumstances.

Many times the characters are involved in more than one conflict, though one struggle will usually dominate. Jacob, the main character in Genesis 27-35, struggles against his brother, Esau, and his father-in-law, Laban (man against man). However, as the plot develops, it becomes increasingly clear that his main conflict is with God (man against a greater power). The story of Jacob reaches its climax when his struggle against God actually becomes physical (Gen. 32:22-32).

The central characters will be either **protagonists** or **antagonists.** The protagonist (Greek, "the chief struggler") is the main character. In a sense the narrative is his story, for the action in the plot shows how this person struggles and conquers or is conquered. Be aware that the protagonist is not always human. In some books God Himself is the main character (e.g., Exodus, Acts, Revelation). The antagonist ("the struggler against") opposes the protagonist and embodies either partially or entirely the conflict that the main character faces. The antagonist may be a person or a force.

Often in books that cover a comparatively brief time span, there will be only one set of protagonists and antagonists (e.g., Ruth, Nehemiah, Job). Books that cover several centuries cannot, of course, have a single human protagonist. Such books present several main characters that come and go with the passage of time (e.g., Genesis, Judges, I and II Kings).

Structure

The biblical storyteller carefully selects and structures the narrative's conflict to give it a clear sense of progression toward a resolution. Any story will be structured with a beginning (the point at which the conflict begins), a middle (a moment of crisis), and an end (the resolution of the conflict). Most stories, however, evidence a more thorough structure. The most common plot pattern involves seven key elements. Though you may not be familiar with the following terms, you will probably recognize the ideas they represent. Since the story of the Exodus (Exod. 1:1-15:21) well illustrates these elements in action, we will use this narrative to help us understand plot structure.

The Book of Genesis ends with the children of Israel enjoying a highly favored status in Egypt. The story of the Exodus, however, takes place in a very different situation. Therefore, the narrator introduces this story with a lengthy **exposition** (Exod. 1-4). In these chapters he lays the foundation for the story by introducing the central characters (God, Moses, and Pharaoh) and the conflict. The exposition ends with an **inciting moment,** which sets the conflict of the plot in motion. When Pharaoh flatly refuses God's order to "let my people go," the battle commences (Exod. 5:1-2). Once the conflict has begun, the narrator relates many confrontations and horrific miracles (Exod. 5:3–12:28), which progressively grow in intensity, moving toward a climax. This series of events is called the story's **rising action.** The rising action culminates in a climactic incident called the **crisis moment** (Exod. 12:29-32). At this point the outcome of the conflict becomes clear. When the death angel kills every firstborn Egyptian, and Pharaoh exclaims, "Rise up, and get you forth" (Exod. 12:31), we no longer have any reason to doubt who will win this war.

In many narratives the crisis moment is also the turning point in the plot. With such stories the rising action records the triumph of the protagonist (or sometimes the antagonist), but the climax records a reversal. Throughout the rising action of Judges 13-16, Samson, the protagonist, remains victorious over his antagonists, the Philistines. At the crisis moment, however, when he reveals the secret of his strength to Delilah (Judges 16:16-20), Samson becomes a defeated hero whose tragic fate is sealed.

After the crisis moment, the narrator records the activities resulting from the climax—Israel's leaving Egypt and traveling to the Red Sea. This series of events is called the **falling action,** which prepares us for the resolution. Often the falling action ends with a **moment of final suspense.** In the story of the Exodus, we encounter the final suspense when Pharaoh and his army attack the Israelites at the Red Sea (Exod. 14:5-18). In the ensuing **denouement** (French, "an untying") the narrator unravels the various "knots" that remain in the conflict by recording how God parted the Red Sea and destroyed the Egyptians. The denouement

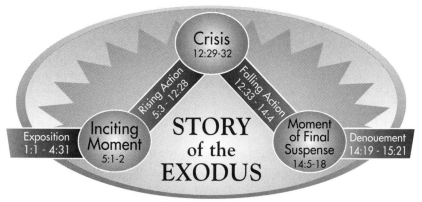

fittingly closes this story of intense conflict with the joyful praise of God's relieved people (Exod. 15:1-21).

We must be sensitive to plot structure and conflict as we explore the meaning of biblical narratives. By observing these elements we will break away from the chapter-a-day mentality, which parcels up a single, connected story into small, seemingly independent units. Exodus 1-15, for example, is not a work of fifteen separate daily readings. It is a single story involving several characters struggling for a resolution to their conflict. We must realize that the narrative as a whole communicates a message, and that message is the primary point the author is trying to make. As we look for meaning in the smaller units of the story, we can do so legitimately only by relating those smaller units to the overall conflict and structure of the plot. If we neglect analyzing the plot, we most likely will make major points out of minor ones or, worse, misunderstand the point of the whole story.

Character

The characters of a narrative make the story come to life. Through characterization the narrator often teaches the reader how to live, and the examples that he produces from history are so real they become the reader's friends (or enemies). To understand the narrator's message, you must get to know the characters to the fullest extent that the information in the story will let you.

Kinds of Characters

As you examine the story's characters, you will find that most of them can be categorized as **sympathetic** or **unsympathetic.** A sympathetic character is one who wins the reader's sympathy, whereas an unsympathetic character does not. As we read the story, we find ourselves effortlessly "cheering" for the sympathetic characters—excited when they win a conflict, disappointed when they are defeated. Often a reader can correctly determine which characters are sympathetic simply by asking, "Who would I like to be in this story?"

Usually the protagonist will be a sympathetic character and the antagonist will be unsympathetic. However, this generalization certainly is not always the case. I Kings 16-22, which records the reign of Ahab, is a fine example. Although this king is the central character for this section of the book, one quickly becomes so disgusted with the man's wicked deeds that a reader is not even tempted to sympathize with Ahab. In the end, when Ahab dies in battle (I Kings 22:34-35), the reader feels satisfied that good has triumphed over evil.

Often a sympathetic protagonist will function in the story as a *normative character.* Such a character presents a positive example of how God wants the reader to live. Not everything the person does, however, is a divine mandate. Rather, God intends that only certain *incidents* in the life of a normative character be exemplary. For example, David, one of the most famous normative characters, teaches the reader a number of lessons about loyalty, obedience, trust, and zeal. However, at times he presents a negative example in each of those categories.

Of course, the best example of a normative character (one without any faults) is the character of Jesus Christ. Our Lord Himself invited people to imitate His life: "Take my yoke upon you, and learn of me; for I am meek and lowly in heart: and ye shall find rest unto your souls" (Matt. 11:29). Later in the New Testament, the apostle John solemnly confirms Christ's words, "He that saith he abideth in [Christ] ought himself also so to walk, even as he walked" (I John 2:6).

The amount and kind of information that an author records about a person will determine whether that character is perceived as **round** or **flat.** Flat characters are so called because they are two-dimensional. Their actions are so consistent that they never surprise us. Round characters, however, are more complex and therefore appear three-dimensional. The notorious pair, Ahab and Jezebel, provide a good example of the difference between round and flat characters. Jezebel plays a significant role in I and II Kings. However, the narrator records her actual words on only three occasions, and on one of those occasions her speech amounts to just one sentence (I Kings 19:2). Furthermore, whenever we read about her, she is behaving wickedly, without any remorse. Ahab, on the other hand, is more complex. We know a great deal more about him than we do his wife, and sometimes his actions and words surprise us. Although he is portrayed as a determined, capable monarch, we once find him behaving like a spoiled little child (I Kings 21:4-7). And though he lives in rebellion to God's Word, he does at times evidence some remorse and a fear of God (I Kings 20:42-43; 21:27-29).

The narrator also presents **dynamic** and **static** characters. Static characters do not change throughout the story. The action of the plot happens *to* them but not *in* them. A dynamic character, however, is one who changes. The conflict he encounters does not remain external; it moves inside his soul and makes him a different person. In the Book of Exodus, Pharaoh encounters many conflicts but never experiences a change of heart. Moses, on the other hand, develops dramatically. He begins as a self-confident leader but soon is crushed by opposition (Exod. 2). After his flight from Egypt, he is so broken that he initially refuses God's supernatural call to deliver Israel (Exod. 3-4). Nevertheless, through the succeeding chapters we watch this man once again become an effective leader—no longer self-confident but God-dependent (note especially Deut. 34:10-12).

The pervasiveness of dynamic characters in biblical narrative is designed to encourage us. In these books we find that God has regularly used difficult circumstances to meet people's most basic need—change. Surely the reason He has preserved so many accounts of inward triumph is that He intends to accomplish the same work in our lives as well.

Methods of Revealing Characters

Occasionally, the biblical author will reveal the nature of character *directly.* Usually the narrator will introduce a character with a few statements of character **description.** Sometimes the narrator will insert such direct descriptions throughout the narrative as well. Notice how the following inserted description shapes our understanding of Moses' character.

> And Miriam and Aaron spake against Moses. . . . And they said, Hath the Lord indeed spoken only by Moses? hath he not spoken also by us? And the Lord heard it. *(Now the man Moses was very meek, above all the men*

which were upon the face of the earth.) And the Lord
spake suddenly unto Moses, and unto Aaron, and unto
Miriam, Come out ye three unto the tabernacle.

—Numbers 12:1-4 (italics added)

Much more frequently, the narrator *indirectly* reveals what the
characters are like. Sometimes we learn about the characters
through their **action.** Thus David's response in the grip of a severe trial is an eloquent testimony to how we should view him.

And David was greatly distressed; for the people spake of
stoning him, because the soul of all the people was
grieved, every man for his sons and for his daughters: *but
David encouraged himself in the Lord his God.*

—I Samuel 30:6 (italics added)

Most often, however, biblical narrators reveal character
through **dialogue.** This dialogue may come from the *speech of
others.* Our first insights into David's character come through
such dialogue—and as the story unfolds we find that every word
of this characterization is accurate.

And Saul said unto his servants,
Provide me now a man that can
play well, and bring him to me.
Then answered one of the servants, and said, *Behold, I have
seen a son of Jesse the Beth-
lehemite, that is cunning in playing, and a mighty valiant man,
and a man of war, and prudent
in matters, and a comely person
and the Lord is with him.*

—I Samuel 16:17-18
(italics added)

What Would You Say?

Certain portions of Scripture
imply the reason God prefers to
use dialogue to reveal a person's
character. Examine the following
references. Can you discern the
reason that dialogue is the Bible's
preferred method of characterization?

1. I Samuel 16:7
2. Matthew 12:34
3. Matthew 12:37

The most common revelatory dia-
logue is the *character's own speech.* Whereas modern novelists
tend to describe characters through extended, detailed appraisals
of their physical appearance, biblical narrative gives little attention

to the characters' looks but heavily emphasizes their words. Recall how much of the previous quotation from Exodus 5-6 (pp. 76-77) was dialogue. In that passage the narrator—without himself saying anything about Moses, Pharaoh, or Jehovah—paints a clear portrait of each person by presenting each person's words.

Setting

A story's setting is the backdrop for its action. As the narrator tells his story, the setting functions as a "container" appropriate for the events and characters of the narrative. Part of the narrator's craft is to omit certain elements of the historical background and emphasize others in order to highlight the significance of the events recorded. The narrator is not deceiving the reader when he does so. Just as there are certain factors in the events of any day that are more significant than others, so certain elements in the setting of a historical event are more important than others for understanding God's working in the world. Under inspiration the narrator followed God's direction concerning which items should be emphasized and therefore described in varying degrees of detail. If the reader will develop a careful eye for noticing the details of setting, he will greatly enhance his ability to discern the lessons God intends all readers to glean from biblical narratives.

What Would You Say?

If you doubt that the biblical historians did indeed carefully select what elements of setting to include or exclude, compare Genesis 17:1-22 with Genesis 18:1-33. Side by side, these chapters describe two similar days in the life of Abraham. But the narrator's careful portrayal of each day's setting gives the two days very different effects in the narrative. Read these chapters and see if you can detect the reason these days are described so differently.

The **physical setting** consists primarily of the story's placement geographically. This includes the topography of the region in which the action takes place, the climate, the buildings, and other similar details. Notice how the physical setting contributes to the meaning of the following paragraph.

And by the hands of the apostles were many signs and wonders wrought among the people; (and they were all with one accord *in Solomon's porch*. And of the rest durst no man join himself to them: but the people magnified them. And believers were the more added to the Lord, multitudes both of men and women. . . . Then the high priest rose up, and all they that were with him, . . . and were filled with indignation.

—Acts 5:12-14, 17 (italics added)

The phrase "in Solomon's porch" identifies for the reader the place where the early church regularly met. The author inserts this important description to explain why many Jews feared joining the church. They knew that becoming a Christian meant continu-ally being identified with Jesus in the very precincts where His death was plotted. But the church still grew, and thus this detail about Solomon's porch also emphasizes the fact that the church's continued growth was nothing short of miraculous. The physical set-ting in this passage also helps explain the reason that the high priest, the administrator of the entire temple complex (and chief conspirator in Jesus' death), envied and feared the apostles' popularity.

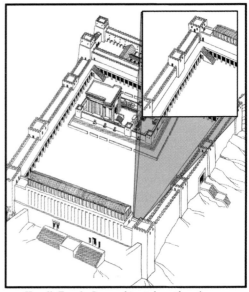

Herod's Temple–*Reversed inset shows the colonnade known as "Solomon's porch."*

The **temporal setting** con-cerns the placement of the story in time. The narrator may develop a *broad temporal setting* (a period in history or a stage in the character's life) as well as a *narrow temporal setting* (the day of the week, season of the year, or even time of day). Note the importance of a broad temporal setting in the introduction to the story of Ruth.

Now it came to pass *in the days when the judges ruled,* that there was a famine in the land. And a certain man of Bethlehem-judah went to sojourn in the country of Moab, he, and his wife, and his two sons.

—Ruth 1:1 (italics added)

By informing the reader that this story takes place during the period in Israel's history characterized by lawlessness and foreign invasions (Judg. 21:25), the narrator prepares us to appreciate more fully the significance of the events we are about to encounter.

Finally, narrators usually interact with a **cultural setting.** This setting is composed of the customs and way of life characteristic of the civilization to which the characters belong. The reader must pay careful attention to these details because they help to explain actions and statements in the story that would otherwise seem strange or meaningless. To the modern reader, God's prohibition, "Thou shalt have no other gods before me" (Exod. 20:3), sounds unnecessary, and perhaps even ridiculous. "Why would the Israelites want to worship more than one God?" we may be tempted to ask as we read. However, if you carefully note the cultural setting for Genesis and Exodus, you soon discover that idols were as common then as telephones are today. Furthermore, trusting those gods for security and prosperity was deemed as necessary as having a steady income. By commanding His people to worship Him alone, Jehovah was calling Israel to make a clean break from all other cultures. This understanding of the cultural setting helps the reader appreciate the importance of the first commandment. One also discovers the reason it was so frequently disobeyed.

Explore a Narrative

Once you have chosen the book, or narrative within a book, that you want to study, you will need to read the text at least twice. Each time try to read the entire story in one sitting. Though this will be difficult with longer narratives, it will pay rich dividends. As you do these readings, you may want to consider working with an edition of the Bible that prints the text in paragraph form. This format should help you read the text as a unified story, not as a listing of independent verses.

The first time through, you should simply observe what is happening. The only notes you should make at this point should concern words or phrases you do not understand. Initially search for the answer to such questions by looking up those verses in a modern version. If that approach does not answer your questions, you should examine these verses in some commentaries at a later point.

The second time through you will need to give more attention to detail. Jot down who you think the protagonists and antagonists are and try to state in one sentence the overall conflict. Next, you should mark out the general plot structure by noting the inciting moment (the beginning), the crisis or climax (the middle), and the resolution (the end). Once you have made these observations, you are well on your way to answering the six key questions for exploring the narrative.

Where and When

The *where* and *when* of a narrative concern the physical setting *(where)* as well as the temporal and cultural settings *(when)*. As you probably observed from the examples in the previous section, biblical historians usually refer to details of setting without explaining them. This fact should not surprise us since the author was communicating, in most cases, to an audience familiar with the settings of his story. Since, however, we are not as familiar with that ancient world, we must use several tools designed to give us the familiarity that the author assumed his readers possessed.

Bible atlases give good insights into the physical setting. Most Bibles have a small set of maps in the back that can be helpful. However, this information is extremely abbreviated and therefore

GET THE BIG PICTURE

I.   Setting Analysis—*Where, When*
II. Character Analysis—*Who*
III. Plot Structure Analysis—*What*
IV. Purpose Analysis—*Why*
V.   Artistic Analysis—*How*

often will not answer your questions about the physical setting. For this reason you should use a full-length Bible atlas. Such a tool not only gives more detailed information with each map but it also contains many maps of the same geographic regions, showing how certain places changed over time. Many Bible atlases also contain a number of artists' renderings of key buildings and the layout of certain cities. As you comb through the text again, use the atlas to identify every location in the narrative— whether a nation, a city, or a particular building—and jot down in your study journal the significance, if any, of these locations. Some of the locations, of course, will be too small or particular to be included in the atlas (a person's house, or a certain field). In such cases you should examine the text itself for clues concerning the significance of these places.

When dealing with questions of cultural setting, Bible dictionaries, encyclopedias, and commentaries offer helpful insights. As you work with the text, take note of statements or actions that seem strange or without apparent motivation. Often such strangeness indicates an allusion to the story's cultural setting. To answer questions of cultural setting, check the explanations of the problematic verse in some commentaries. If the explanations there do not seem adequate, look up the cultural element mentioned in the narrative in a Bible dictionary or encyclopedia.

Finally, as you read the narrative, take note of the temporal setting. Consider the broad temporal setting for the narrative as a whole, as well as the narrow temporal setting for each scene in the story. Commentaries can be very helpful with this material. Note especially what the introductory sections in the commentaries say about the broad temporal setting. Again, be sure to write down the observations that you find significant.

Who

By this point you should have already identified the protagonist and antagonist. Now you will need to investigate the characters more thoroughly. Reserve a place in your study journal for the protagonist, the antagonist (if it is a person), and the supporting characters. Then describe each character using the terminology discussed earlier (sympathetic, unsympathetic, dynamic, static, and so forth). As you study the characters, remember that narrators sometimes reveal insights about their characters through direct description, more often by actions, and most often through dialogue. Take special note of any dynamic characters, whose lives remind us that God's grace does change people.

You should also be sensitive to the presence of a normative character. Legitimately identifying such a character is a significant step toward discerning the meaning of a story. As you look for the normative character(s), keep in mind that the key indicator of such a character is *rewarded choice*. When the narrator shows that a character's choices lead to ultimate triumph, the author is most likely highlighting those choices as exemplary behavior.

What

Now that you have identified the main characters and their conflicts, you are ready to explore the plot's structure. Mark in your Bible as many of the seven classic elements of plot structure (see pp. 80-81) as are present in the narrative. Then sketch a diagram of the plot in your study journal.

Once you have divided the text into plot elements, you should read through the exposition, rising action, falling action, and denouement. Usually these sections will be composed of several, or many, *scenes* that help to introduce, intensify, or resolve the story's conflict. Each scene will be unified by a single event and will often contain a brief introduction and conclusion. Usually, the author will signal the end of a scene by changing the characters, the setting, or both. You should identify each of these scenes by marking them in the text with lines. Then you can briefly summarize in the margin what happens in each scene. Once you have summarized these smaller units, you can then summarize the larger units: exposition, rising action, falling action, and denouement. Based on the summaries of these larger units—as well as your summaries of the inciting moment, the crisis, and the final suspense—you can formulate in one sentence a description of what happens in the entire narrative.

Why

"There are also many other things which Jesus did, the which, if they should be written every one, I suppose that even the world itself could not contain the books that should be written" (John 21:25). The apostle John, like all historians, was faced with a dilemma as he prepared to write his Gospel. On the one hand, he desired to communicate clearly the significance of his subject, the person and work of Jesus Christ. But he knew that physical constraints would not permit him to include all the information available. John 20:31 suggests that the apostle solved this dilemma through **thematic selection.** He chose a particular theological point to develop, and then he selected the incidents that most clearly demonstrated that point. Therefore, every scene in the Gospel of John was carefully chosen to contribute to the key theme: "Jesus is the Christ, the Son of God" (John 20:31).

If we will fully appreciate the enduring message of John's Gospel—or any historical book—we must constantly ask why each event was included. Why, for example, does this apostle begin his record in eternity past, describing Christ's communion with the Father and His creation of the world (1:1-3)? Furthermore, why does John skip the birth account of Jesus and present Him for the first time in His humanity at the beginning of His ministry (1:29ff)? Such questions shape, correct, and sharpen our understanding of the main theological message (as well as the various subthemes) of any historical book.

Why, however, involves more than investigating the author's thematic selection. We must also explore **narrative emphasis.** Not every detail in a biblical story is equally important. Certain scenes, descriptions, speeches, and conversations are much more significant to the author's message. Generally, narrators emphasize the key elements by giving them more space. Again, consider John's Gospel. In just twenty-one chapters, John reveals the work of Jesus Christ from eternity past through some of His post-resurrection appearances. In the first eleven chapters, he moves from the creation of the world through most of Christ's earthly ministry. The next nine chapters record the events of *one week.* Out of those nine chapters, seven concern just twenty-four hours of that week. Clearly, if we wish to understand thoroughly what the Gospel of John is all about, we must ask ourselves why this one week, with its climactic day, is so important to John's message.

Therefore, as you study a narrative, explore the author's thematic selection by jotting down the reason you think that each scene has been included. After lengthy scenes, try to formulate the reason the author saw fit to emphasize those events. Taking time to account for the author's selection and emphasis is a powerful tool for correcting and enhancing your understanding of the narrator's enduring theological message.

How

In all of our detailed analysis, we must never forget that the authors of biblical narrative were literary artists. They were concerned not only to convey a message but also to delight the reader with beauty. Such a concern for artistry allows the story to address the reader's entire being—not just his intellect. When we experience the beauty of a story, our emotions become involved in the reading process. Thus the story moves beyond information and becomes persuasion. As we study these historical books, we should take time to note three common classes of narrative artistry that give the stories their powerful "punch."

The biblical storytellers frequently lace the rising action with **mystery,** which is the withholding of important information from the reader. If the narrator openly withholds information, he creates *suspense,* thus making the reader's interest keener. *Surprise,* on the other hand, is achieved by secretly withholding information from the reader. An interesting example of both kinds of mystery is found in I Kings 3:16-28. This passage records a legal dilemma presented to King Solomon. Two women stood before him, each claiming to be the mother of the same baby. While the women make their pleas, the narrator purposefully withholds any hint of the resolution Solomon is pondering, thus keeping us in suspense as we read. When, however, Solomon commands, "Divide the child in two" (I Kings 3:25), suspense quickly becomes a setup for surprise. When only one of the women cries out in protest, Solomon replies, "Give her the living child, . . .

THE SECOND BOOK OF MOSES, CALLED

EXODUS

Israelites prosper
(to introduce Israel's threat to the Egyptians)

Israelites grow despite enslavement
(to introduce Israel's predicament)

Israelites grow despite murder
(to foreshadow God's conflict with Pharaoh)

Now these are the names of the children of Israel, which came into Egypt; every man and his household came with Jacob.

2 Reuben, Simeon, Levi, and Judah,

3 Is´sachar, Zebulun, and Benjamin,

4 Dan, and Naph´tali, Gad, and Asher.

5 And all the souls that came out of the loins of Jacob were seventy souls: for Joseph was in Egypt already.

6 And Joseph died, and all his brethren, and all that generation.

7 And the children of Israel were fruitful, and increased abundantly, and multiplied, and waxed exceeding mighty; and the land was filled with them.

8 Now there arose up a new king over Egypt, which knew not Joseph.

9 And he said unto his people, Behold, the people of the children of Israel are more and mightier than we:

10 Come on, let us deal wisely with them; lest they multiply, and it come to pass, that, when there falleth out any war, they join also unto our enemies, and fight against us, and so get them up out of the land.

11 Therefore they did set over them taskmasters to afflict them with their burdens. And they built for Pharaoh treasure cities, Pi´thom and Ra-am´ses.

12 But the more they afflicted them, the more they multiplied and grew. And they were grieved because of the children of Israel.

13 And the Egyptians made the children of Israel to serve with rigour:

14 And they made their lives bitter with hard bondage, in morter, and in brick, and in all manner of service in the field: all their service, wherein they made them serve, was with rigour.

15 And the king of Egypt spake to the Hebrew midwives, of which the name of the one was Shiph´rah, and the name of the other Pu´ah:

16 And he said, When ye do the office of a midwife to the Hebrew women, and see them upon the stools; if it be a son, then ye shall kill him: but if it be a daughter, then she shall live.

17 But the midwives feared God, and did not as the king of Egypt commanded them, but saved the men children alive.

18 And the king of Egypt called for the midwives, and said unto them, Why have ye done this thing, and have saved the men children alive?

19 And the midwives said unto Pharaoh, Because the Hebrew women are not as the Egyptian women; for they are lively, and are delivered ere the midwives come in unto them.

20 Therefore God dealt well with the midwives: and the people multiplied, and waxed very mighty.

21 And it came to pass, because the midwives feared God, that he made them houses.

22 And Pharaoh charged all his people, saying, Every son that is born ye shall cast into the river, and every daughter ye shall save alive.

[for] she is the mother" (v. 27). Then we realize that we are the happy victims of artful surprise.

This scene functions in the Solomon narrative to demonstrate that this king's wisdom was incomparable. Though simply stating, "Solomon's wisdom was incomparable," could have communicated the same message, such a simple statement would not have possessed the same power. Because of the narrator's masterful use of suspense and surprise, this episode is one of the best known in the Old Testament.

Sometimes the narrator places his reader in the privileged position of **enlightenment.** This artistic tool may take the form of *foreshadowing,* an anticipation of the outcome through various kinds of hints. Thus Simeon's final sentence to Mary in Luke 2:35 cryptically and briefly carries the reader forward to the final scenes of Luke's Gospel: "Yea, a sword shall pierce through thy own soul also." Enlightenment may also take the form of *dramatic irony,* which results when the narrator discloses certain facts to the reader that are still hidden from the characters. The Joseph narrative (Gen. 37-50) is one of the most moving stories of biblical narrative primarily because of dramatic irony. As we watch the brothers ignorantly paying homage to the brother they thought they had killed, we find ourselves amazed that they unwittingly are fulfilling the prophecy they had been determined to thwart. When the irony reaches its climax with Joseph's long-awaited words, "I am Joseph," the reader *feels* the triumph of God's gracious providence, rather than simply reading about it.

Finally, we should carefully note the narrative's use of **recurrence.** If the narrator presents an event or a statement more than once with little or no variation, he is employing *repetition.* If, on the other hand, he repeats a statement or event with significant variation, he may be using *contrast.* Repetition and contrast work effectively together in the story of Creation (Gen. 1). In verses 1-25 the repetition of God's command, "Let there be" or "Let [something happen]," occurs eleven times, giving the narrative a majestic cadence artistically appropriate for this display of the Lord's omnipotence. But in verse 26 the narrative startles the reader with a contrast, "Let *us* make man." This contrast in wording sets man apart as the climax of God's creation.

Final Words

The narrative genre can combine all the other genres within itself. Often the narrator will include letters and poems, as well as other less common literary types. Consequently, the reader must be alert and ready to "switch gears" from one genre to another while reading a narrative. Once he analyzes the different components of such a narrative, he must assemble the results of his investigation by asking how that letter or poem relates to the details of the story in which it is found.

After you have worked through the narrative, be sure to record your findings. You should have made some notes on each of the six questions in your study journal. Record the most significant of these observations in your Bible. In your Bible you should also mark the various scenes throughout the story (including the summaries and purpose statements), identify the elements of plot structure applicable to this narrative, state the conflict, list the main characters, and write down the one-sentence summary statement for the narrative.

Review Questions

True or False

Write *T* in the blank if the statement accurately reflects the content of this chapter and *F* if it does not.

_____1. The Bible is primarily a book of history.

_____2. The story of Jacob (Gen. 27-35) is about a man torn by one struggle.

_____3. Round characters are those that experience inward change throughout the story.

_____4. When the narrator omits certain elements of the historical setting as he describes the setting in the story, he is making the significance of the historical events and people he describes clearer.

_____5. When the narrator employs *recurrence,* he is usually making use of *foreshadowing* or *dramatic irony.*

Multiple Choice

Choose the answer that best represents the content of this chapter.

_____6. The historical books of the Bible can best be described as

    A. historical chronicles of the nation of Israel.
    B. a collection of fanciful fairy tales.
    C. an anthology of folk epics.
    D. a series of literary narratives.

_____7. What will most likely happen if we neglect plot analysis while exploring a biblical narrative?

   A. We will not know where to begin in our analysis of the author's message.
   B. We will make major points out of minor ones, and we may misunderstand the message of the story.
   C. The role of each character will become more plain.
   D. We will have difficulty applying the narrative.

_____8. The most common indicator that someone in a narrative is a normative character is the presence of

   A. a direct commendation by God.
   B. a direct commendation by the narrator.
   C. rewarded choice.

_____9. Dramatic irony results when the author

   A. creates a sense of suspense in the story.
   B. withholds information from the reader that the characters possessed.
   C. discloses certain facts to the reader that are unknown to the characters.
   D. anticipates the outcome of the story through various kinds of hints.

Short Answer

10. What do you think is the main reason God has chosen to record history in the genre that dominates the historical books?

11. What are the three key elements of any story?

12. Structured conflict is the essence of what element in a story?

13. Define thematic selection.

14. How does the Bible differ from secular history books?

15. Describe the most common kind of plot structure.

16. What are the common ways in which a narrator reveals to the reader the nature of the story's characters?

17. On your own paper, identify as many of the seven elements of plot as you can find in John 9. Try to identify the protagonists and antagonists, as well as the nature of the scene's conflict. On the basis of those observations, summarize in one sentence what this episode is about.

Project

Following the suggestions outlined in this chapter, explore the narrative that your teacher assigns.

CHAPTER SIX

Apply!—Finding the Way of the Word

6

II Timothy 3:16-17

Is Application OK?

College was proving to be quite a challenge for Martin. His mind was probably equal to the task, but his soul was in turmoil. He was attending a Christian college and was interested in spiritual things. But as the school year progressed, he became increasingly distressed. He wanted to know God, but he didn't know how to go about it. Repeatedly he had been told in his classes and in chapel that God speaks through the Bible. Martin, however, knew better than to believe that idea. "The Bible was not written to me," he reasoned. "The real recipients of those books are now long gone. If I found something significant for my life in one of those ancient books, I'd be a weirdo getting comfort from reading somebody else's mail." One morning he went to a prayer room to pour out his heart to God: "O Lord," he prayed, "please speak to me." Nothing happened. Again he prayed, "Show me Yourself!" Silence. "I'll take an angel, Lord," he finally pleaded—still no voice from heaven. Disgusted and discouraged, he walked out of the room convinced that he would never hear from God.

Much to his surprise, however, Martin got what he wanted only a few hours later—though not in the form he was expecting. While he was sitting in chapel listening to an ordinary message, the speaker said something that arrested his thoughts—and his heart: "Some people are so arrogant that they expect God to speak to them in an audible voice." Then he realized that it was

not his "commitment to truth" that had made him doubt the applicability of Scripture. It was pride.

Martin's pride had not only kept him from God, it had blinded him to the clear statements of Scripture. The Bible is not "somebody else's mail." The Scripture itself affirms that it is the Word of God: "All scripture is given by inspiration of God" (II Tim. 3:16). And because it is God's message to man, all of it is presently applicable "for doctrine, for reproof, for correction, for instruction in righteousness." For this reason the apostle Paul freely used passages more than 1,000 years old to meet the spiritual needs of his contemporaries (e.g., I Cor. 10:1-14). He, as an inspired author of Scripture, was so confident in the Bible's present applicability that he absolutely affirmed, "Whatsoever things were written aforetime were written for our learning, that we through patience and comfort of the scriptures might have hope" (Rom. 15:4). But not only is it *possible* to apply the Scriptures, it is *necessary*. James told his readers that they were obligated to apply and obey the Word of God: "Be ye doers of the word, and not hearers only, deceiving your own selves" (James 1:22). Though an ancient book written originally for people now long-since dead, the Bible is God's ordained means of speaking to believers in each generation.

Therefore, we must not stop interpreting when we finish exploring the meaning of Scripture. We need to use that ancient meaning to find God's path for us today. We cannot say that we have properly interpreted a passage until we have discovered how its meaning is significant for our lives. We must apply the Word. However, we need to be careful to develop proper applications. Indeed, not all applications are created equal—some are downright sinful.

When Satan tempted our Lord, he first enticed Him to use His supernatural power to satisfy His hunger. But Christ repelled him by quoting Scripture: "It is written, Man shall not live by bread alone, but by every word that proceedeth out of the mouth of God" (Matt. 4:4; Deut. 8:3). Defeated by the ultimate authority, Satan then retreated and tried another tactic. "If thou be the Son of God," he said, "cast thyself down [from the pinnacle of the temple]: for it is written, He shall give his angels charge concerning thee: and their hands shall bear thee up" (Matt. 4:6; Ps. 91:11-12).

Recognizing that the Scripture was Christ's defense, the Devil took the words of God, and—without twisting the meaning of those words—applied them to Christ's situation. But, as the context of Matthew 4 makes clear, if our Lord had obeyed that application of Scripture, He would have *sinned.*

Finding Parallels

Satan's use of Psalm 91:11-12 was not a legitimate application because certain key elements in that psalm were not parallel to Christ's situation. Psalm 91 does discuss God's miraculous protection. However, verse 11 is a promise to God's people who are thrust into perils beyond their control. If such people are submitted to God and relying on Him (v. 9), the Lord promises to see them through their trials. But since Christ was experiencing no such trials, His obeying Satan would have been reckless abandon, and He would have been siding with Satan against the Lord. Such a violation of God's will would have invalidated the promise of deliverance. But Christ, our model of godliness in temptation (and in application), saw through Satan's trick and quoted another verse that *was* parallel to His situation: "It is written again, Thou shalt not tempt the Lord thy God" (Matt. 4:7; Deut. 6:16).

If you carefully observe Christ's example, you realize that legitimate application is essentially *finding the present demands of*

Scripture by discerning the parallels between the text and your life. We must constantly look at what we have learned from our biblical explorations and compare them to our situation—all the while looking to God (the Author of the text) to help us see the parallels. Good application, therefore, requires a three-pronged knowledge: knowing the text, knowing God, and knowing yourself.

SCRIPTURE   CHRISTIAN

Knowing the Text

Your ability to apply the Scripture will be influenced by how well you have explored its meaning. For the last four chapters, we have been learning how to do exegesis. If you have "hung in there" until now, you know enough about the texts you have studied to be one-third of your way to sound applications. As you apply, you will regularly draw on the answers to all six questions *(where, when, who, what, why,* and *how)*. However, the *what* answers—shaped, developed, and corrected by the other five—will usually contain your most valuable conclusions.

Knowing God

As you may have guessed, knowing God is the most important "prong" for application. If you are not a child of God—one who knows God and is known by God—the legitimate parallels between the text and your life will seem unremarkable at best and nonsensical at worst. Knowing how the text applies to everyday life is knowledge that is "spiritually discerned" (I Cor. 2:14). To see these parallels clearly requires that the Spirit of God commune with the believer's spirit. *He* convinces the Christian that the parallels are real, and that they must be obeyed. If a person does not know God, he "receiveth not the things of the Spirit of God: for they are foolishness unto him" (I Cor. 2:14).

How do you know that you know God? A good answer to that question is another question: does God's Spirit speak to your spirit as you read the Word? If the pages of Scripture consistently seem dry and inapplicable to you, you may simply lack the capacity to receive and enjoy spiritual communication—you may not be saved. However, as you have no doubt heard hundreds of times, if you are not a Christian, you can become one right now. God can work the greatest miracle known to man in your soul, even while you are reading this book. What does He ask you to do? He is looking for you to submit to the gospel: "If thou shalt confess with thy mouth the Lord Jesus and shalt believe in thine heart that God hath raised him from the dead, thou shalt be saved" (Rom. 10:9). To be saved you must accept Jesus as your Lord and trust entirely in His sacrifice for you. Such believing people receive much more than a home in heaven. God pours out His Spirit on them, and they are supernaturally enabled to see how the Word applies to them.

Knowing Yourself

Finally, you must know yourself. Since each person is different, the number of legitimate applications for a given passage will be multiple, though the meaning of the text is always singular. Knowing yourself in application may seem obvious at first. After all, what possibly could we know better than ourselves? But we need to remember that we are complex, wicked beings. The Lord Himself said, "The heart is deceitful above all things, and desperately wicked: who can know it?" (Jer. 17:9). Such a judgment may seem to make our study hopeless, but God assures us in the next verse, "I the Lord search the heart." The extent of our sinfulness

---

A Prayer for Application

Break Thou the bread of life,
Dear Lord, to me,
As Thou didst break the loaves
Beside the sea;
Beyond the sacred page
I seek Thee, Lord,
My spirit pants for Thee,
O living Word.

Bless Thou the truth, dear Lord,
To me, to me,
As Thou didst bless the bread
By Galilee;
Then shall all bondage cease,
All fetters fall;
And I shall find my peace,
My All in all.

—Mary Lathbury (1841-1913)

is beyond our ability to perceive, but God knows. As we apply the Word, we must ask Him to show us our needs.

Apostolic Application

Before we progress further, we should take a few moments to examine an extended example of an inspired application. In I Corinthians 10:1-14, the apostle Paul applies narratives from Exodus and Numbers, which concern Israel in the wilderness. Paul assumes that these Old Testament narratives concern people and events that are "ensamples," which have been recorded "for our admonition" (I Cor. 10:11). Based on that legitimate assumption, he looks for parallels between the Corinthian believers and the Israelites. He first notes that both have received special privileges from God (vv. 1-4). Just as these Christians had enjoyed baptism and the Lord's Supper, Israel had been "baptized" by passing through the Red Sea and had been fed by divine food and drink (manna and water from the rock). Second, he observes that Israel was "overthrown in the wilderness," and that the Corinthians were in danger of a similar disaster (vv. 5-6). On the basis of these two parallels, the apostle warns them not to behave the way that the Israelites did. Specifically, he exhorts them not to be idolaters, not to commit fornication, not to tempt Christ, and not to complain against God's provisions and dealings (vv. 7-10).

From this authoritative example, we can extract three principles for applying narratives. First, assume that the book you are

ISRAELITES	CORINTHIAN BELIEVERS
Descendants of Abraham	
Privileged to cross the Red Sea on dry ground	Privileged to be baptized in God's name
A nation called to conquer the Promised Land	
Privileged to enjoy miraculous food and water	Privileged to partake of the Lord's Supper
Delivered from Egypt miraculously	
Complained against God's provisions	Tempted to complain
Led by Moses for forty years	
Guilty of idolatry and fornication	Tempted to be idolatrous and commit fornication
Struggling while journeying through the desert	
Destroyed in the desert	Based on these parallels, in danger of judgment

reading presents parallels for believers today. Second, after exploring the text, look for parallels between the text and your life. Usually this amounts to finding which characters, events, or situations are similar to you or your particular experiences. Third, on the basis of those parallels, decide what action you should take. In the example above, once Paul had established that the Corinthians were similar to the Israelites in the wilderness, the application was obvious: don't commit the sins they committed so that you won't face the punishment they experienced.

Genre and Application

Just as the genre of a book determines how we explore it, so the genre is a key consideration while applying the truth. The remainder of this chapter will discuss various guidelines for application in the three main biblical genres.

 ### Application in the Epistles

Parallels

The parallels between the reader and the text in the New Testament epistles are more extensive than in any other genre. The apostles were addressing men and women in our situation: the people of God gathered out of the world serving Him in the church. Therefore, you will notice, first of all, many parallels **between the author and yourself.** You can learn from the author's *positive example* by seeking to emulate his exemplary deeds, thought patterns, and prayer life. Naturally, however, there are certain limitations to these parallels due to the fact that an apostle's calling differs from ours. So Paul's announcement that he needed to visit Rome and then travel to Spain with the gospel ought not be taken as a normative example for us to follow (Rom.15:24). He was God's apostle to the Gentiles, and we are not. The most extensive parallels in the epistles exist **between the recipients and you.** The major applicable elements here are *commands*. You are to obey the author's commands concerning actions, thoughts, and beliefs.

Occasional Elements

The interpreter must still exercise caution, however, for there are some commands in the epistles that do not carry over as normative. These inapplicable statements exist primarily because the epistles are *occasional documents*—they were originally written to a particular group of people whose exact situation was unique. Consequently certain elements in the text were meant for the recipients only, or for Christians in that time only. We all recognize the enduring significance of the command, "Be strong in the grace that is in Christ Jesus" (II Tim. 2:1). But what about another command that occurs only two chapters later: "Do thy diligence to come before winter" (II Tim. 4:21)? Consider the book of Philemon. The major commands in that book concern forgiving Onesimus. Are we to obey those commands? If so, how?

Before you reach for a commentary in such situations, be aware that modern scholarship tends to lump too much of the text in the "occasional" category. The dangers of going overboard in this regard are serious: you may end up dismissing part of God's contemporary message as irrelevant. To avoid this danger while applying the epistles, you should assume the text is directly applicable unless the epistle itself, or history, demonstrates otherwise. The epistle will let you know that the command is occasional if the action prescribed is so limited in applicability that it is impossible for you to perform it. For example, Paul's request for Timothy to visit him before winter is so particular that it cannot be obeyed now, two thousand years later.

Information from history can also help us in this regard. If a command in an epistle concerns the

What Would You Say?

A recurring debate in biblical interpretation concerns some commands that Paul gave in I Corinthians 11:1-16. This passage is problematic for two reasons. First, it is difficult to discern whether the apostle was instructing the Corinthian women to wear a head covering during worship or to refrain from cutting their hair. Second—and more importantly—many disagree about the passage's applicability. Do Paul's commands to female believers apply only to the original readers of I Corinthians 11? Read the passage for yourself. Using the guidelines given in this chapter, try to answer this question of applicability.

proper use of an ancient custom that does not exist in our culture, the instruction probably is not directly applicable. For example, I Thessalonians 5:26 charges the saints to "greet all the brethren with an holy kiss." If you were to follow this command at your next prayer meeting, it would do more than turn a few heads. And well it should, for God does not intend that you kiss the brethren. History teaches us that in the ancient Near East a "peck on the cheek" was a common way to greet a person. Paul's command cannot be directly applied to our situation because the kind of greeting that Paul was sanctifying does not exist in our culture.

Yet even the occasional elements in a biblical letter are in a sense applicable because they do teach us something about God and Christians. For example, in II Timothy 4:13 Paul instructed Timothy, "The cloke that I left at Troas with Carpus, when thou comest, bring with thee, and the books, but especially the parchments." Though these commands are not directly applicable, they are indirectly. The verse reminds us that even an apostle needs the help of fellow believers (bringing the coat). Furthermore, we learn that even someone of Paul's spiritual stature (and physical station—near death) should endeavor to learn more about the Scriptures.

 ## Application in the Psalms

Parallels

He prayed and we must pray—this statement expresses the chief parallel between the psalmist and Christians today. We, along with Christ's disciples, longingly sigh, "Lord, teach us to pray" (Luke 11:1). And, though the Bible teaches us principles of prayer from cover to cover, nowhere is the teaching so instructive as in the Psalms. This collection of 150 poems gives us *patterns for worship*. Therefore, you should note the **themes** of these poems and incorporate them into your prayer life. As the author reflects on God's greatness and goodness, he is giving us a pattern to follow. When he searches for spiritual restoration after failure, his words teach us what we should do to recover from defeat. The more familiar you get with the various themes in the

Psalms, the more capable you will become at expressing yourself to God effectively.

More than just themes, the interpreter must also recognize the parallels in **manner of worship**. Perhaps knowing *how* to approach God is just as important as knowing what to say. The Book of Psalms instructs us here as well. The psalmist's attitudes and verbal demeanor should be emulated. Sometimes that demeanor will surprise you (e.g., Ps. 10:1), and consistently it will challenge you to be biblical in the way you worship and pray to your Lord.

Worshiping with the Psalms

Perhaps the best way to apply the psalms is to use them in worship. When you spend time in Bible study and prayer, take some time every day to pray to the Lord a psalm. Sometimes you will be praising him and sometimes making requests, but always you will be communicating with Him according to His will, for you will be speaking to Him with His own words. If you have a copy of the Psalms set to music, sing God's Word back to Him.

Problems in Applying the Psalms

I'm not an Israelite!—Some of the material in the Psalms will seem inappropriate for your prayers because it is nationalistic. Originally the Book of Psalms served as Israel's hymnbook. Therefore, common themes include military victory, national stability, removal of sinful leaders, and the restoration of national prosperity. Since our role in God's plan for the ages does not involve being a nation that conquers and maintains land, none of these

What Would You Say?

"He that goeth forth and weepeth, bearing precious seed, shall doubtless come again with rejoicing, bringing his sheaves with him" (Ps. 126:6). This verse has often been cited as a proof text for God's blessing on witnessing. Accordingly, the going forth refers to confronting people with the gospel, the seed is the Word of God, and the sheaves represent converted sinners. However, this interpretation does not account for what the text meant to its original audience—it skips exegesis. Why do you suppose that such an obvious misinterpretation has become so popular? What do you think Psalm 126:6 means? Is that meaning applicable to witnessing for Christ?

themes is directly applicable to our lives. Each of these, however, is still indirectly applicable in at least four ways.

First, such nationalistic themes teach us how a nation should behave. If David was burdened to pray that God would give Solomon divine wisdom to rule Israel (Ps. 72), we ought to be burdened to pray the same for our leaders. When Asaph in Psalm 79 mourns that Jerusalem has been sacked because of its sin (cf. II Chron. 12:2-12), we should reflect on the fact that national sin brings national disaster. Surely if God did not spare His chosen people, He will punish any wicked nation.

Second, these elements in the Psalms remind us of the importance of Israel in God's plan. In Psalm 89 Ethan reminds the Lord of His unshakable promise: "[David's] seed also will I make to endure for ever, and his throne as the days of heaven" (Ps. 89:29). This psalm with its many pleas for national restoration should teach us that God's promises to Israel are at the center of His program for this earth. How He will work out this plan may be beyond us, but we must keep Israel's importance in the front of our minds by praying with the psalmist, "Lord, where are thy former lovingkindnesses, which thou swarest unto David in thy truth?" (Ps. 89:49). Such a prayer may seem inapplicable to the modern American because he cannot see how God's answering that prayer can directly affect him. However, we need to learn that effective praying involves supplicating for needs far beyond our own interests. Since these requests are of great importance to God, they should be important to us as well. Praying for things that do not affect us but do accomplish the glory of the Lord shows that we truly are concerned for the chief end of man.

Third, since any nation is a collection of individuals, those national sins that are condemned in the Psalms are condemned on the personal level as well. Conversely, whatever virtues are praised are virtues that individuals should add to their personal lives.

Finally, this devotion to Israelite nationalism should remind us of the devotion that we must evidence for God's purposes. During the theocracy of Israel, God's purpose for His people was that they subdue the land and occupy it in righteousness. Christ has called us, on the other hand, to spread His gospel "unto the uttermost part of the earth" (Acts 1:8). Therefore, as the psalmist cries for help that the theocracy may continue and fulfill its divine mandate, we should reflect on redoubling our efforts and prayers to "teach all nations" the gospel of saving grace (Matt. 28:19).

Impre—what?!—Certain psalms trouble Christians because they contain imprecations (curses prayed against enemies). Such prayers seem scandalous in the light of Christ's clear command to "love your enemies" (Matt. 5:44). But before anyone rashly concludes that these prayers are somehow "beneath" New Testament revelation, he should consider that even the apostles cursed their enemies (Acts 8:20; Gal. 1:9; 5:12). And one day in heaven glorified saints will pray imprecations before God's throne (Rev. 6:10).

Nevertheless, an important question remains: how can such prayers be reconciled with Christ's command to love? The answer is found in the life of David. This man is the chief author of imprecatory statements in the Psalms. Yet his life is exemplary in his willingness to forgive enemies. His foes are notorious in Scripture: Saul, Nabal, Absalom, and Shimei. However, he refused to seek vengeance on any of these men. The key to his victory over bitterness and revenge lies in his imprecations. Through these prayers David released the responsibility for seeking vengeance into God's hands. Thus he was free to seek the good of his enemies because he knew that getting justice in these situations was no longer his concern. As you read these imprecations, reflect on your own life. Have you been wronged? In the words of the psalmist, deliver vengeance into God's hands, and leave it there.

DID YOU KNOW?

The Imprecatory Psalms
Although imprecations are found throughout the Psalms, four psalms are thoroughly imprecatory. Such psalms are simply extended curses prayed against the psalmists' enemies: Psalms 35, 69, 109, and 137.

Application in the Narratives

Certainly it would be easier to interpret the historical books if after each narrative the author appended: "The moral of this story is _____." However, such a blunt approach would both spoil the artfulness of the stories and discourage thorough study. The biblical narratives teach spiritual lessons through their use of plot, character, and setting. Because the biblical narrators communicate their "morals" in a subtle manner, mistakes often abound when applying. These mistakes occur so frequently that some have even despaired that the historical books are not applicable—particularly the ones with long genealogies! However, God has assured us that every passage of Scripture is profitable (II Tim. 3:16-17). If we will take the time to learn how to recognize legitimate parallels, we will discover that God's promise of applicability is true—even in the historical books.

Avoid Allegorizing

Allegorizing is the arbitrary assigning of spiritual meaning to every detail of a narrative. For example, in the story of Gideon's attack on the Midianites (Judg. 7:16-25), one may allegorize the text by stating that the story teaches the believer how to have victory over sin. The Midianites are Satan's hordes, who tempt us daily. To defeat them we must take our clay pitchers (our physical desires) and break them in surrender. Then we must let our lamps (Christian testimony) shine. At the same time, we should use our swords to fight the Midianites (quoting Scripture in the time of temptation). Thus our supernatural tempters will flee from us in fright.

The problem with this method of application is that it is not based on any serious attempt to explore the passage. Thus, it is dangerously subjective. With this approach one could just as easily conclude that Gideon's victory teaches us that we should arm ourselves against any hostile government, kill our personal enemies, or even homestead in Israel's West Bank with tanks and guns. If the parallel we seek to draw between our lives and the Scripture is not based on sound exegesis, our applications will most likely come from our own imagination—not the mind of God.

Avoid Personalizing

Personalizing results from assuming that every detail within a narrative is directly applicable to one's life. Whereas allegorizing is flawed because it is based on bad exegesis, personalizing is flawed because it does not discriminate between the elements in the text that are not parallel and those that are. While it is true that every passage of Scripture does somehow apply to us, not all of it directly applies and some details do not apply at all.

An extreme example of personalizing would be some people's application of I Samuel 25:39-42. In this passage David marries a second wife, Abigail. Therefore, some men have reasoned that they too may have more than one wife. However, such an application fails to consider the fact that what *happened* in the text is not always what *should* have happened. And if something should not have happened in Bible times, it should not happen today either. Since the Bible elsewhere opposes polygamy (Deut. 17:14-17; I Tim. 3:1-2), this particular detail in I Samuel cannot be a positive example. Legitimate applications do not violate clear statements in Scripture.

Focus on Wholes

As you seek to discriminate between details that are applicable and those that are not, you must focus on the story as a whole. Often Bible students make incorrect applications because they fail to recognize the fundamental difference between the epistles and the narratives. Many of the biblical letters are theological treatises and are therefore packed with enduring spiritual lessons and observations. One could legitimately preach for a year on just Romans 8. (Some have!) Biblical narratives, on the other hand, communicate spiritual truth in an expanded form. Characteristically, a narrative communicates only one major lesson to the reader, though it will teach various related minor lessons along the way. The student of Scripture must first determine what that enduring message is before he can confidently apply the book, and its various parts, to his life.

During the *what* stage of narrative study, you formulated a one-sentence summary statement for the entire narrative. To apply that statement, you need to express the summary as a timeless truth. For example, when we read Daniel 1, we learn that in 605 B.C. God preserved and blessed Daniel and his friends because they obeyed, even in great adversity. But if we meditate on these events, we realize a more powerful, enduring truth about God (the theological message): "The Lord preserves and blesses His people who are submitted to Him, no matter how difficult their circumstances are." How particularly you should apply this theological message depends on your own situation. If you are experiencing a severe trial and are submitted to the Lord, this narrative applies to you as a reminder that God will take care of you. If, however, you are not submitted to Him and experiencing adversity, the story should convict you about your uncertain future because of your sin.

Focus on the Narrator's Comments

As we noted in Chapter 5, the biblical narrators develop the characters and events of their stories primarily through dialogue and straightforward descriptions of events. However, occasionally the author will change his mode and give a brief commentary on the spiritual significance of an event or person. Such statements are gold mines for application.

For example, in the middle of the genealogies found in I Chronicles 1-9, the narrator switches from recorder to exhorter as he states the significance of the life of an otherwise unknown figure from the conquest of Canaan. "Jabez was more honourable than his brethren. . . . [He] called on the God of Israel, saying, Oh that thou wouldest bless me indeed. . . . And God granted him that which he requested" (I Chron. 4:9-10). From these sentences we learn that we too should fervently ask for God's blessing on us. The reader cannot go wrong focusing on such statements for application because by them the author himself is applying the text to the reader.

Focus on Rewarded Choices

As we apply narratives we should also look for rewarded choices. When the narrator shows how a particular choice led a person to triumph and blessing, he is giving us an example to follow. The reverse, however, is also true. If we observe that a choice leads to destruction, we should note that deed as a sin to avoid.

Gospel Narratives

Finally, applying the Gospel narratives presents a unique challenge to the believer. Since the Gospels concern a very different figure, Jesus Christ, there exists a pronounced *two-level communication* that is not as prevalent elsewhere in biblical narrative. Our Lord never sinned (I Pet. 2:22). And though His primary purpose for coming to earth was to die for our sins, He also came to show us what God the Father is like (John 1:18). Therefore, all that Christ says and does is an important part of the Bible's theological message. Yet, the narrator's message speaks with authority as well. The point of a particular scene may not be the same as the point of a speech or interchange from Christ, but the point of both are still valuable and applicable.

For example, consider Matthew's use of the Sermon on the Mount (Matt. 5-7). The theme of Matthew's Gospel is that Jesus of Nazareth is the Messiah-King. His purpose in recording the Sermon on the Mount was to demonstrate Christ's kingly authority by showing the authority of His teaching. But if we focus on that point alone for application, we will miss many important lessons. Within that demonstration of authoritative teaching, we can find a wealth of spiritual lessons by which we must live. Therefore while reading the Gospels, continue to focus on the narrative as a whole, but be sure to give special attention to the deeds and teachings of Christ.

Conclusion

God's firm path for your life will clearly emerge if you properly apply His Word. As you discern applications for your life, tell your parents and pastor about the steps you believe God is leading you to take. They will not only confirm and correct your handling of the Word but will also keep you accountable for stepping into the path of obedience that God reveals to you.

Review Questions

Write *T* in the blank if the statement accurately reflects the content of this chapter and *F* if it does not.

_____1. While applying the text, you will find that your *how* conclusions will be the most valuable.

_____2. Out of the three "prongs" of knowledge necessary for proper application, the most important is knowing the text.

_____3. *Personalizing* results from assuming that every detail within a narrative is somehow directly applicable to one's life.

Choose the answer that best represents the content of this chapter.

_____4. Why was Satan's application of Psalm 91:11 illegitimate?

   A. He twisted the plain meaning of the words.
   B. Certain key elements in the psalm were not parallel to Christ's situation.
   C. His application stood in direct contradiction to various commands in Leviticus.
   D. Satan cannot properly apply the Scripture because he is a fallen creature.

_____5. When applying the epistles, you will find that the key parallel between yourself and the author is

    A. his commands.

    B. his personal history.

    C. the cultural background of his world.

    D. his positive example.

_____6. The epistles contain many occasional elements, which cannot be applied directly to our lives. How should we determine which elements are occasional and which are not?

    A. Assume the text is directly applicable unless the text itself or history demonstrates otherwise.

    B. Assume the text is not applicable unless the context demonstrates that it must be.

    C. Follow the advice of commentaries.

    D. Assume any statement that applied to the culture of the original readers must not be applicable to us.

Short Answer

7. What does legitimate application involve?

8. Which of the three major genres is most applicable to believers today?

9. What is perhaps the best way to apply the Psalms?

10. Define allegorizing.

11. How do we know that the Bible is God's Word for believers in each generation?

12. How does I Corinthians 10:1-14 help us understand the nature of proper application?

13. Read Psalm 122. Apply this psalm by using two principles of application discussed in this chapter.

14. Read Esther 1:1–3:6 and then analyze the following statement: "Esther 1 teaches us the vital importance of women living in complete submission to their husbands."

15. How do the Gospel narratives differ from other narratives in their applicability?

CHAPTER SEVEN

Obey!—Following the Way of the Word

7

Matthew 7:7-12

Determination?

You've explored the meaning of Scripture; you've figured out how it applies to your life—now what? Follow the path that God has shown you in His Word. How do you do that? Determination. You just decide that you are going to obey the Word, and then you do it. God's commands are not difficult. Anyone can obey them. *Or can he?*

What words come to mind when you hear the name Benjamin Franklin? Inventor, statesman, insightful writer, printer, philosopher—an impressive list. In the history of the United States of America, there are very few people as successful as this man. It seems that whatever he undertook, he mastered. As one author has said, Franklin "was an American who set an example for other Americans by constantly testing the resources of his mind and character." *Character,* yes—that seems to have been his strength. Benjamin Franklin accomplished so much because he possessed the determination necessary to succeed. Franklin himself, however, shows a different opinion in his *Autobiography.*

It was about this time [around 1730] I conceived the bold and arduous project of arriving at moral perfection. I wished to live without committing any fault at any time; I would conquer all that either natural inclination, custom, or company might lead me into. . . .

In the various enumerations of the moral virtues I had met with in my reading, I found the catalogue more or less numerous . . . . I included under thirteen names of virtues all that at that time occurred to me as necessary or desirable, and annexed to each a short precept, which fully expressed the extent I gave to its meaning. . . .

Conceiving God to be the fountain of wisdom, I thought it right and necessary to solicit his assistance for obtaining it; to this end I formed [a] little prayer . . . for daily use.

My list of virtues contained at first but twelve; but a Quaker friend having kindly informed me that I was generally thought proud . . . that I was not content with being in the right when discussing any point, but was overbearing and rather insolent, of which he convinced me by mentioning several instances; I determined endeavoring to cure myself, if I could, of this vice or folly among the rest, and I added Humility to my list.

I cannot boast of much success in acquiring the *reality* of this virtue, but I had a good deal with regard to the *appearance* of it. . . .

In reality, there is, perhaps, no one of our natural passions so hard to subdue as *pride.* Disguise it, struggle with it, beat it down, stifle it, mortify it as much as one pleases, it is still alive, and will every now and then peep out and show itself; you will see it, perhaps, often in this history [his *Autobiography*]; for, even if I could conceive that I had completely overcome it, I should probably be proud of my humility.

In the same work Franklin lists many other virtues he desired but could never acquire. The moral failure of such a great man should teach us an important lesson about our race. Without the grace of Jesus Christ, humans cannot be virtuous—they cannot obey God. But Franklin prayed for God's help. Doesn't such devotion indicate that he was depending on God for that grace? To help you better understand Franklin's situation, consider some statements he made in a letter shortly before he died.

> As to Jesus of Nazareth, my Opinion of whom you particularly desire, I think the System of Morals and his Religion, as he left them to us, the best the World ever saw or is likely to see; but I apprehend it has received various corrupting Changes, and I have . . . some Doubts as to his Divinity; tho' it is a question I do not dogmatize upon, having never studied it, and think it needless to busy myself with it now, when I expect soon an Opportunity of knowing the Truth with less Trouble. I see no harm, however, in its being believed, if that Belief has the good Consequence, as probably it has, of making his Doctrines more respected and better observed.

Franklin could not be victorious over sin because his unbelief had cut him off from the only Source of true victory. Thus he could fight sin only in his own strength—a strength unequal to the task. But if you are born again, you possess a supernatural ability that Benjamin Franklin never enjoyed. To discover that power, however, you must know and embrace what the Bible says about you, your salvation, and the promises of God.

What You're Made Of

In all that He does, God seeks to glorify Himself (Rom. 11:36). For the sake of displaying His unique excellence, He created us in His own image. But when Adam disobeyed, that image was marred and so was our ability to imitate and glorify the Lord. Though Adam had rejected God's perfect will, the Lord promised to reverse our sad state by sending a Savior (Gen. 3:15). At the appointed time He, the Son of God, came as a human being and perfectly obeyed God's law. But when He could have claimed His right to eternal life as a sinless human being, He instead surrendered to the Father's will by suffering on the cross. Christ became the substitute for all sinners, bearing in His body God's wrath for our sins. Because of Christ's sacrifice, God now delivers from the Fall everyone who believes the gospel. By reversing the Fall and its curse, God makes believers like His own Son (Rom. 8:29).

Thus He enables us to fulfill our original purpose—proclaiming God's excellence by imitating Him.

God's work in restoring that image, however, is a *process*—one that begins with regeneration and continues through sanctification. The moment you were saved, God reconstructed your inner being and made you a "new man" (Eph. 4:24; Col. 3:10). In this miraculous work, called **regeneration,** God effected at least three changes. First, He freed you from the control of the "flesh" by mysteriously uniting you with Jesus Christ in His death (Rom. 6:4, 6-7). Therefore, just as the guilt that Christ bore on the cross could not affect Him once He was dead, so sin can no longer control you, a person who died to sin with Christ. Second, God gave you new life. He made you a "partaker of the divine nature" (II Pet. 1:4), giving you a set of new spiritual desires and abilities that correspond to His own perfect character. The Lord brought this "new you" to life by spiritually uniting you with Christ in His resurrection that first Easter morning. Thus just as our resurrected Lord lives today in complete submission to the Father, so every believer is free to serve God (Rom. 6:4-10; Gal. 2:20). Finally, in regeneration God placed His Holy Spirit in your heart (Rom. 8:9, 11-12).

MASTER the TERMS

Regeneration: the instantaneous change wrought by God in a believer's life at conversion that involves the dethroning of the flesh, the bringing to life of a new nature, and the indwelling of the Holy Spirit (sometimes called the *new birth*)

Old man: all that a person is before conversion (could be translated "former man")

New man: all that a person is after conversion

Flesh: the composite of evil inclinations and capacities that human beings have inherited from Adam (sometimes called the *old nature* or the *sin nature*)

Sanctification: the process by which the believer becomes less like the old man and more like Jesus Christ

Amazingly, these miracles happened in a moment of time—the moment you trusted Christ. "But when I got saved," perhaps you're wondering, "I didn't *feel* anything like that." Just because you don't notice an action doesn't mean it hasn't happened. You can't really "feel" protein synthesis or a series of nerve impulses, but both are happening in abundance right now while you read this book. From your perspective you simply repented of your sin and believed on Christ. But from God's perspective you were at that time being united with Christ at Calvary, being buried with Him in the garden, being raised up from the tomb, and being indwelled by His Holy Spirit.

Considering the marvelous miracle of regeneration brings us to an important question: if God's work in saving us is so extensive, why do we still struggle with sin? The answer is found in two words—*the flesh.* Though our union with Christ breaks the grip of the flesh, God has seen fit to let that flesh remain in our inner being.

The Struggle Within

Sanctification is the process by which the believer becomes less like the person he was before conversion (his "old man," Rom. 6:6; Eph. 4:22) and more like Jesus Christ. By growing in sanctification the believer enjoys the most rewarding process that anyone can know in this life. But this growth comes through struggle, and with that struggle comes frustration. The apostle Paul frankly confessed the frustration that all

DEVOTED TO GOD

HOLY SPIRIT

FLESH

ABLE TO OBEY

The New Man

believers feel in sanctification: "The flesh lusteth against the Spirit, and the Spirit against the flesh: and these are contrary the one to the other: so that ye cannot do the things that ye would" (Gal. 5:17). This constant internal conflict between God's desires and those of the flesh can so frustrate the believer that he begins to despair of ever living in peaceful obedience. To such believers, God's law seems like a five-ton weight, whose multitudinous commands crush all hope and joy.

God's Well-Worn Path

Is there no hope then? Does God's gracious salvation amount to nothing more than this struggle? The previous paragraph quotes Galatians 5:17. Now consider the next verse: "But if ye be led of the Spirit, ye are not under the law." This sentence cannot mean that we may freely disobey God's law. The following verses reiterate the importance of God's moral code. Rather, the apostle Paul is stating here that God has designed a way for us to please Him with joy. If we follow His plan, we can live in obedience to His Word without experiencing the frustration of the flesh's conflict with God's will.

In a phrase, victory over sin and frustration comes by "walking in the Spirit" or "being led by the Spirit" (Rom. 8:14; Gal. 5:16, 18). The simple command to walk in the Spirit soothes the frustration that burns in the believer's soul. Our call to sanctification is not a sentence to lifelong misery. The Christian life can and ought to be one of inner tranquility and victory. To discover that victory, we need to do only one thing: *submit to God's Spirit moment by*

Think About It! We must be careful not to separate the Spirit's leading from the Word of God. Sometimes people attribute their bad decisions and even cruel actions to "the mysterious leading of the Spirit." God's Spirit, however, will never lead us contrary to the Word He has written. In fact, the Bible is the Spirit's primary means of guiding believers. For this reason the apostle Paul, comparing the Word to a mirror ("glass" KJV), states that as we are guided by the Bible, the Spirit is leading us toward Christlikeness. "But we all, with open face beholding as in a glass the glory of the Lord, are changed into the same image from glory to glory, even as by the Spirit of the Lord" (II Cor. 3:18).

moment. If we try to obey the Lord by focusing on His many commands, we will not defeat the flesh. Knowing our weakness, God has called us to seek victory by simply letting the Spirit lead.

To be sure, He will lead us to obey God's law, but He will do so through a *relationship.* Lovingly, God's Spirit will give us all that we need to live in victory. He can tell us what God's will is because He knows what God desires, and He lives in our hearts (Rom. 8:11). He will also help us do what is right because He has promised to empower us. Though sanctification is a battle, it is a battle fought by following the gentle guidance of our loving friend—the Holy Spirit of Jesus Christ. Though we will stumble along the way, He will always be with us to help us up and lead us back to victory. As we live each day, our minds should not be filled with hundreds of spiritual obligations to remember and do. At any given time, God asks of us only one thing—follow the Spirit.

Learning to Walk

If you're like me, your faith is small. You know that simply trusting God's Spirit and obeying Him will lead to victory over sin, but your personal experience of failure cripples your confidence. Even now as you meditate over these truths, perhaps you can hear a discouraged voice echoing in your soul, "God *has* given me everything I need to be victorious. I believe that. But what if I don't have the strength to take advantage of what He's given? What then?"

In the Sermon on the Mount (Matt. 5-7), our Lord called His disciples to obey the spirit of God's laws. Adultery, He warned, was not limited to sexual misconduct. Adulterous thoughts are just as certainly sinful as adulterous acts. He also told them that if they wanted to be innocent of murder, they could not even hate their fellow man. Furthermore, He challenged them not to think that the command "love thy neighbor" refers only to one's friends. That command meant they must love their enemies too. These teachings are only a few of the maxims that He gave that day. By the end of the sermon, the disciples probably felt crushed by God's colossal expectations.

But as Christ was concluding His sermon, He revealed the secret for finding the power to obey: "Ask, and it shall be given you; seek, and ye shall find; knock, and it shall be opened unto you" (Matt. 7:7). God gives His strength to those who ask for it. How do we know, you may be wondering, that the thing asked for in that verse is victory over sin? Notice how Christ concludes His discussion of asking and receiving: "Therefore all things whatsoever ye would that men should do to you, do ye even so to them: for this is the law and the prophets" (Matt. 7:12). Since this "asking passage" concludes with an exhortation to obey the law and the prophets, *ask-seek-knock* must refer primarily to praying for the ability to obey God's Word. *Ask for victory*, Christ says, *and you'll have it.*

We must realize, however, that this is a particular kind of asking. The verbs *ask, seek,* and *knock* could more literally be translated *keep asking, keep seeking,* and *keep knocking.* The Lord Jesus, therefore, was telling His disciples to request persistently the grace for obedience.

If you are a converted person, but you are not walking in God's path, you need to renew your fight in sanctification by beginning where Christ concluded His Sermon on the Mount—*pray!* Daily plead with Him to give you the grace to obey the Spirit moment by moment. When you fail, submit again to the Spirit and *pray.* When you're tempted to conclude that you'll never change, submit and *pray.* When everything inside of you screams, "Give up!" *PRAY!* Since there is a God in heaven who always keeps His promises, you can rest assured that you will experience the power of the Holy Spirit. And as you begin discovering that power, continue praying. Never stop praying for God's grace to keep flowing into your soul.

Think About It!

Do not let doubt quench the work of God in your life. Remember that the Lord longs to answer your persistently asked requests—even more than you desire to see them answered. Listen to words of His own Son: "What man is there of you, whom if his son ask bread, will he give him a stone? . . . If ye then, being evil, know how to give good gifts unto your children, how much more shall your Father which is in heaven give good things to them that ask him?" (Matt. 7:9, 11).

Never suppose, however, that God will answer such a prayer by removing all temptation. The Lord allows temptation and the flesh to remain in your life so that He may test your love and commitment to Him. What you can count on, though, is the power of God to carry you through the temptation to obedience.

"Take up the ark of the covenant," Joshua told the priests as all the Israelites stood before the Jordan River. "When ye are come to the brink of the water of Jordan, ye shall stand still in Jordan" (Josh. 3:6, 8). This was no small command. It was the time of year that the Jordan overflowed its banks and rushed with a dangerous current. Nevertheless, God's words were clear. There was no chance that the priests had "misexegeted" or misapplied the command. Jehovah's path for them lay within those impossible waters. Ignoring their fears, the priests chose to believe the Lord, and down to the water they went. It was not within their power to cross the river, but it was their responsibility to enter the flood. Then "as they that bare the ark were come unto Jordan, and the feet of the priests that bare the ark were dipped in the brim of the water, . . . the waters which came down from above stood and rose up upon an heap" (vv. 15-16). That day God called His people to agree to do the impossible, and once they agreed, He did the impossible. "And all the Israelites passed over on dry ground" (v. 17).

So it is for you. No matter how hard you pray, you must still "get your feet wet." You must trust God to the point of obeying. Then God's grace will become obvious. Though covered by the flood of your flesh and past failures, God's seemingly impossible path will at that point become plain and safe. You know what God wants, and you know that you can trust Him . . . *now walk!*

Review Questions

Write *T* in the blank if the statement accurately reflects the content of this chapter and *F* if it does not.

_____1. God's commands are not difficult.

_____2. Though it can be challenging to remember all of God's commands throughout the day, we may rest assured that since such concentration is part of God's plan for sanctification, we are able to keep all those commands in mind.

_____3. When Christ commanded His disciples to "ask, and it shall be given," He was referring to praying for something persistently—not a single, one-time prayer.

Short Answer

4. Define what the word *flesh* means biblically.

5. Define the term *sanctification.*

6. Describe the events that take place in regeneration.

7. Explain what the following statement means—and does not mean: "If ye be led of the Spirit, ye are not under the law."

8. Why does Matthew 7:7 seem to refer primarily to asking for victory over sin?

Photograph Credits

The following agencies and individuals have furnished materials to meet the photographic needs of this textbook. We wish to express our gratitude to them for their important contribution.

Andover Newton Theological School
The British Museum
Corel Corporation
Franklin Trask Library
Library of Congress
Photo Disc, Inc.
Unusual Films
www.arttoday.com

Title Page
  Photo Disc, Inc.

Chapter 1
  Unusual Films 4; Library of Congress 11;
    www.arttoday.com 13

Chapter 2
  Corel Corporation 23 (background);
    Courtesy of Franklin Trask Library,
    Andover Newton Theological School 24

Chapter 3
  The British Museum 35

Chapter 6
  www.arttoday.com 105

Chapter 7
  www.arttoday.com 125, 133